THE EIGHT KINGDOM PARABLES

THE EIGHT KINGDOM PARABLES

Craig Munro

40 Beansburn, Kilmarnock, Scotland

ISBN-13: 978 1 912522 94 1

Copyright © 2020 by John Ritchie Ltd.
40 Beansburn, Kilmarnock, Scotland

www.ritchiechristianmedia.co.uk

All rights reserved. No part of this publication may be reproduced, stored in a retrievable system, or transmitted in any form or by any other means – electronic, mechanical, photocopy, recording or otherwise – without prior permission of the copyright owner.

Typeset by John Ritchie Ltd., Kilmarnock
Printed by Bell & Bain Ltd., Glasgow

CONTENTS

Foreword			7
Introduction			9
Chapter 1		The King and Kingdom in Matthew	11
Chapter 2		The Kingdom of God in the Past	17
Chapter 3		Thy Kingdom of God in the Future	23
Chapter 4		The Kingdom in Mystery in the Present	35
Chapter 5		The Kingdom in the Tribulation	43
Chapter 6		The Kingdom Parables – Why Parables?	55
Chapter 7	Parable 1	The Sower	63
Chapter 8	Parable 2	The Wheat and Tares	73
Chapter 9	Parable 3	The Mustard Seed	83
Chapter 10	Parable 4	The Leaven in the Meal	91
Chapter 11	Parable 5	The Treasure in the Field	99
Chapter 12	Parable 6	The Pearl of Great Price	107
Chapter 13	Parable 7	The Drag Net	117
Chapter 14	Parable 8	The Householder's Treasure	125
Conclusion			131

Appendix 1	Seven Transforming Changes that will take place in the Millennial Kingdom	135
Appendix 2	Seven Reasons why the Church will not go through the Tribulation	139
Chart	The Second Coming of Christ for the Church and for Judgment upon Earth	148
Appendix 3	The Subtle Difference between the Kingdom of God and the Kingdom of Heaven	149

FOREWORD

This is the third of a series that Craig Munro has undertaken, dealing with familiar Bible topics. He first covered 'The *Ten* Commandments' and then 'The *Nine* Beatitudes'. He now covers 'The *Eight* Kingdom Parables'. Eight Kingdom Parables! Are we not accustomed to speaking of "The *Seven* Parables of the Kingdom" in Matthew 13? Craig contends that the reference to the householder at v.52 should be included, and so he speaks of eight parables.

The teaching Craig gives in this book is more or less in line with what I learned from men like Mr. David Craig and Mr. Albert Leckie when I was younger; I think it would be regarded as a conservative approach to the subject. He sees the present expression of the Kingdom of Heaven as a sphere of profession in which professing Christians, genuine and spurious, are side by side in the field which is the world.

Although basically doctrinal, the book is incisive in the challenge it presents regarding our commitment to sow seed. Are we employing every avenue open to us to communicate the Word of God? Stress is laid on the fact that it is the only method whereby souls are reached for the Kingdom.

In Matthew 13, the emphasis is on the present manifestation of the Kingdom , but Craig is at pains to stress that in the future there will be a literal physical expression of God's Kingdom when the Lord Jesus will reign for 1000 years, the period that we describe as 'The Millennium'. A helpful appendix is incorporated featuring aspects of that era. Another profitable appendix appears, supplying Biblical reasons to see the Rapture of the Church as an event that precedes the Great Tribulation.

Craig's expositions and conclusions are well backed up with a multitude of Bible references that demonstrate his wide knowledge of the Scriptures, even those parts that we might regard as obscure.

THE EIGHT KINGDOM PARABLES

In his Introduction, Craig suggests that each chapter of his book can be read in five minutes. I recommend that you devote just a little longer to it! If you are going to digest all that is there, and follow up on the Bible references, it will need some diligent thought. I do trust that the little volume will be really enlightening to those of you who are exploring these things for the first time, and an encouraging refresher course for those of you who have known them for many years.

Jack Hay

INTRODUCTION

This book considers the Kingdom Parables told by the Lord Jesus which are collated in one chapter – Matthew 13. This chapter has interested readers of Scripture down through the centuries. Eight short, memorable parables are all clustered together and are often referred to as 'the parables of the Kingdom'.

The purpose of this little book is to encourage the reader to think a little bit more deeply on a familiar section of Scripture. As we study God's Word, we find treasure for our souls. The parables exalt the person of Christ and are the key to understanding the key Kingdom themes of our Bible.

The truth of the Kingdom should be of interest to us all, as subjects of the King. We are *sons of the Kingdom* and a sense of our calling and privilege should grip our souls. The subject of the Kingdom is a vast one, and some explanation of it is required. The introductory chapters of this book deal with the Kingdom of God in its initial and final fulfilment. These chapters also consider the meaning of the Kingdom in the present age, and why the Lord called these parables the 'mysteries of the Kingdom'. The eight parables are then taken up in consecutive chapters. The three appendices give seven features of the changes in the Millennial Kingdom, seven reasons why the Church will not go through the Tribulation and also explain the subtle difference between the expressions the 'Kingdom of Heaven' and the 'Kingdom of God'.

This book is the third published book in a series which tries to deal with a key chapter or section of Scripture. The intention is to publish accessible books on the following key chapters of the Bible:

THE EIGHT KINGDOM PARABLES

1. The 10 Commandments   Exodus 20
2. The 9 Beatitudes   Matthew 5
3. The 8 Kingdom Parables   Matthew 13
4. The 7 Feasts of Jehovah   Leviticus 23
5. The 6 Days of Creation   Genesis 1

Each verse, commandment, beatitude, parable, feast, and day will be expounded briefly, and the chapter will be readable in less than five minutes. At the end of each chapter there is a summary, reflective questions, and a space for notes and personal thoughts on the Scriptures.

All references and Scripture references are placed in a footnote and more detailed information is placed in appendices. The purpose is to allow each chapter to be read quickly, but to provide scriptural evidence for any interpretations given, and to allow readers to explore the subject more fully if they wish to do so.

Reading, meditating, and obeying the Holy Scriptures are the essential elements of a Christian's life. It is hoped that by providing thoughts on these important sections of Scripture in an accessible and concise manner they may be useful for personal study and reflection and perhaps for group/Bible class discussion.

The substance of this book was first published in the *Present Truth* magazine. The material has now been edited further and expanded for this current volume. My simple prayer is that, through publishing this book, the Lord Jesus may be exalted, and God's people built up in their most holy faith. My burden is for a movement in our day back to the Bible with a deeper reverence and obedience to His Word.

Chapter 1

THE KING AND KINGDOM IN MATTHEW

Matthew is the only Gospel that includes all the Kingdom Parables. They are contained in one chapter: Matthew 13. Five of the eight Kingdom Parables are also only found in Matthew's Gospel. The reason for this concentration of parables about the Kingdom and the uniqueness of the material in Matthew's Gospel is because Matthew's Gospel is the 'Kingdom' Gospel. In Matthew the word 'Kingdom' is used 55 times, Mark 20 times, Luke 44 times, and John 5 times. Furthermore, much of the imagery in the book of Matthew is that of a King and his Kingdom. Some of the major chapters concentrating on this theme are listed below:

- Matthew 5-7   Principles of the King and Kingdom
- Matthew 13   Parables of the King and Kingdom
- Matthew 22, 24-25   Prophesies of the King and Kingdom

These three major sections of 'Kingdom' teaching by the Lord Jesus are almost all unique to Matthew's Gospel. Only two chapters in Matthew neglect to mention 'Kingdom' or 'king'. In Matthew alone, the Lord calls Jerusalem, *'the Holy city'*[1] and Jerusalem, *'the City of the great King'*[2].

---

[1] Matt. 4.5: 'Then the devil taketh him up into the holy city, and setteth him on a pinnacle of the temple';
Matt. 27.53: 'And came out of the graves after his resurrection, and went into the holy city, and appeared unto many.'
[2] Matt. 5.35: 'Nor by the earth; for it is his footstool: neither by Jerusalem; for it is the city of the great King.'

THERE ARE SEVEN FEATURES OF THE KING IN MATTHEW:

1. The Purity of the King

*'... of whom was born Jesus, who is called **Christ** (anointed)'*[3]

The Lord Jesus was born of a virgin and did not come from Joseph. This truth is safely guarded in Matthew 1.

2. The Humility of the King

*'Where is he that is **born King**?'*[4].

The Lord Jesus was born in a small insignificant town called Bethlehem as had been predicted by Micah:[5] *'little among the thousands of Judah'*. Although born King, He took the lowest place.

3. The Forgiveness of the King

*'Therefore is the kingdom of heaven likened unto a **certain king**, which would take account of his servants ... I forgave thee all that debt'*[6].

The Lord Jesus was willing to forgive our huge debt of sin. He came to liberate us from the chains of our sins and pay the ransom for our souls: *'Who gave himself a ransom for all'*[7].

4. The Meekness of the King

*'Behold, **thy King** cometh unto thee. Meek ...'*[8].

The Lord Jesus rode in meekness into Jerusalem on a donkey. Although King, He was gentle, wise and never rash in His judgments.

5. The Preparation of the King

*'The kingdom of heaven is like unto a certain **king**, which made a marriage for his son, ... I have prepared ...'*[9].

The marriage supper of the King's Son is a metaphor widely used of

---

3 Matt. 1.1-16 4 Matt. 2.2

5 Micah 5.2: 'But thou, Bethlehem Ephratah, though thou be little among the thousands of Judah, yet out of thee shall he come forth unto me that is to be ruler in Israel; whose goings forth have been from of old, from everlasting.'

THE KING AND KINGDOM IN MATTHEW

❝ *Ultimately, the matter of the King and Kingdom is the crux of the gospel*

the *'marriage supper of the Lamb'* recorded for us in Revelation 19. 9 when the future Kingdom of God will be inaugurated, and peace will be established on earth. *'Blessed are they which are called unto the marriage supper of the Lamb. And he saith unto me, These are the true sayings of God.'*

6. The Judgment of the King

*'Then shall **the king** say ... Come, ye blessed ...'*[10].

This chapter contains the Lord Jesus' own words on His own judgments on people of all nations in a coming day. This tribunal, where all nations appear before Him, is often called the "judgment of the living nations", which will happen immediately after His return to earth to reign as King of Kings and Lord of Lords. His Kingdom will be purged of all things that are offensive and will be marked by righteousness.

7. The Rejection of the King

*'... his accusation written, THIS IS JESUS **THE KING** OF THE JEWS'*[11]

The Lord Jesus was rejected on the cross as King. It really was His claim to be King and the Son of God that was the cause of His rejection by the world. They said: *'We have no king but ...'*[12], and again: *'We have a law, and by our law he ought to die, because he made himself the Son of God'*[13]. Ultimately, the matter of the King and Kingdom is the crux of the gospel. Pilate asked them: *'Shall I crucify your king'*[14] and they refused Him. Pilate asked again: *'What shall I do then with Jesus which is called Christ? They all say unto him: Let him be crucified'*[15]. They then

6 Matt. 18.21-35 7 1 Tim. 2.6 8 Matt. 21.5
9 Matt. 22.2, 4 10 Matt. 25.31-46
11 Matt. 27.27-31, 37 12 John 19.15
13 John 19.7 14 John 19.15 15 Matt. 27.22

shouted: *'His blood be on us, and on our children'*[16]. Israel rejected the King and Kingdom but there were individuals at Calvary who did not. One of them said to Him: *'Lord, remember me when thou comest into thy kingdom'*[17].

Since Matthew is the royal Gospel, we should not be surprised that it tells us more about 'treasure'[18] and gold[19] and coins[20] than any other Gospel.

Furthermore, since it is the Gospel of kingly authority, those who called the Lord Jesus by a name or title in Matthew and thereafter received blessing of any kind only ever called Him *'Lord'*. It is very interesting to compare correlative passages of the four Gospels. When, for example, the disciples are afraid in the storm, they cry to the Lord, 'Master, Master' in Luke's account[21] but in Matthew they call Him *'Lord'*[22]. Luke perhaps emphasises their human fear, Matthew their absolute confidence in the Lord to meet the desperate situation. This is why Matthew shows how Judas is exposed in the Upper Room by his very vocabulary, the way he addresses the Saviour as *'Master'*[23]. Judas never knew Jesus as *Lord*. The blind men in Matthew chapter 9 received no blessing until they learned to call Him *'Lord'*[24]. The angels uniquely say to the women in the garden

---

16 Matt. 27.25 17 Luke 23.42

18 Matt. 6.21: 'For where your treasure is, there will your heart be also';
Matt. 12.35: 'A good man out of the good treasure of the heart bringeth forth good things: and an evil man out of the evil treasure bringeth forth evil things';
Matt. 13.44: 'Again, the kingdom of heaven is like unto treasure hid in a field; the which when a man hath found, he hideth, and for joy thereof goeth and selleth all that he hath, and buyeth that field';
Matt. 13.52: 'Then said he unto them, Therefore every scribe which is instructed unto the kingdom of heaven is like unto a man that is an householder, which bringeth forth out of his treasure things new and old';
Matt. 19.21: 'Jesus said unto him, If thou wilt be perfect, go and sell that thou hast, and give to the poor, and thou shalt have treasure in heaven: and come and follow me.'
19 Matt. 2.11: 'And when they were come into the house, they saw the young child with Mary his mother, and fell down, and worshipped him: and when they had opened their treasures, they presented unto him gifts; gold, and frankincense, and myrrh';
Matt. 10.9: 'Provide neither gold, nor silver, nor brass in your purses';
Matt 23.16: 'Woe unto you, ye blind guides, which say, Whosoever shall swear by the temple, it is nothing; but whosoever shall swear by the gold of the temple, he is a debtor!';

THE KING AND KINGDOM IN MATTHEW

in Matthew's gospel, *'Come, see the place where the Lord lay'*[25]. Matthew, therefore, is the Gospel of the Lordship of Christ in dialogue.

John also emphasises the Lord as king (14 times). John does so to prove His absolute and unrelinquishable position as the Son of God. In Matthew sovereignty, authority, royalty and regal dignity are emphasised; in John deity and superiority are the prime focus. In Matthew we have earth's true king from Heaven who will reign in Heaven and in Earth (28. 18), emphasising His Kingdom 55 times. In John we have Heaven's King on earth, who soon will return to Heaven to be with His Father and then return for His waiting people to take them to Heaven to be with Him.

My Notes

Matt. 23.17: 'Ye fools and blind: for whether is greater, the gold, or the temple that sanctifieth the gold?';
20 Matt. 20.2: 'And when he had agreed with the labourers for a penny a day, he sent them into his vineyard'.
21 Luke 8.24 **22** Matt. 8.25
23 Matt. 26.21-25: 'And as they did eat, he said, Verily I say unto you, that one of you shall betray me. And they were exceeding sorrowful, and began every one of them to say unto him, Lord, is it I? And he answered and said, He that dippeth his hand with me in the dish, the same shall betray me. The Son of man goeth as it is written of him: but woe unto that man by whom the Son of man is betrayed! it had been good for that man if he had not been born. Then Judas, which betrayed him, answered and said, Master, is it I? He said unto him, Thou hast said.'
24 Matt. 9.27-29: 'And when Jesus departed thence, two blind men followed him, crying, and saying, Thou Son of David, have mercy on us. And when he was come into the house, the blind men came to him: and Jesus saith unto them, Believe ye that I am able to do this? They said unto him, Yea, Lord. Then touched he their eyes, saying, According to your faith be it unto you.'
25 Matt. 28.6

THE EIGHT KINGDOM PARABLES

? *What features of the King and Kingdom are revealed in Matthew's Gospel?*

Chapter 2

THE KINGDOM OF GOD IN THE PAST

These parables of the Lord Jesus are called 'Kingdom Parables', but what does that mean? What is the Kingdom? This is a vast truth and it is progressively developed and revealed throughout the Scriptures.

Universal

The Kingdom is the underlying structure of our whole Bible. It is the framework in which the whole of God's revelation is completed, both in creation and redemption. God's Kingdom is the place where the sovereign rule of Christ as King is universal and timeless: '*His kingdom ruleth over all*'[26] and, '*the Lord sitteth King for ever*'[27].

David saw that the Kingdom was much wider than Israel very clearly in his day, exclaiming: '*Thine, O LORD, is the greatness, and the power, and the glory, and the victory, and the majesty: for all that is in the heaven and in the earth is thine; thine is the kingdom, O LORD, and thou art exalted as head above all. Both riches and honour come of thee, and thou reignest over all; and in thine hand is power and might; and in thine hand it is to make great, and to give strength unto all*'[28].

---

26 Psalm 103.19: 'The LORD hath prepared his throne in the heavens; and his kingdom ruleth over all.'
27 Psalm 29.10 **28** 1 Chron. 29.11-12

THE EIGHT KINGDOM PARABLES

In the very early stages of progressive revelation, then, it was known that the Kingdom of God is an *'everlasting kingdom'* and universal,[29] and extends even over all the affairs of the human race, including evil rulers: *'the most high God ruled in the kingdom of men, and that he appointeth over it whomsoever he will'*[30].

Past phase – the choosing of a nation

There were various expressions of the Kingdom of God on earth from the beginning of creation, for example, the garden of Eden with Adam as vice-regent over the earth. There may be other expressions of the Kingdom but one area where we can be sure that the Kingdom of God was seen on earth is in the nation of Israel. God chose a nation to bless the world[31] and explained to Abraham that He would make him the *'father of many nations'* and kings would come out of his loins for an *'everlasting possession'* and based on an *'everlasting covenant'*[32]. The disciples clearly saw Israel as being the Kingdom of God as they asked the Lord, after Rome dominated Israel, whether the Kingdom of God would ever be restored *again* to Israel[33]. The Lord Jesus never disabused them of this thought and it certainly squares with the record of the Old Testament where Jehovah calls Israel *'my kingdom'*[34]. The Psalmist believed this as he sat in the House of the Lord in Jerusalem, crying, *'For the kingdom is the*

---

29 Psalm 145.13: 'Thy kingdom is an everlasting kingdom, and thy dominion endureth throughout all generations.'

30 Dan. 5.21

31 Gen 22.18: 'And in thy seed shall all the nations of the earth be blessed.'

32 Gen. 17. 3-8: 'And Abram fell on his face: and God talked with him, saying, As for me, behold, my covenant is with thee, and thou shalt be a father of many nations. Neither shall thy name any more be called Abram, but thy name shall be Abraham; for a father of many nations have I made thee. And I will make thee exceeding fruitful, and I will make nations of thee, and kings shall come out of thee. And I will establish my covenant between me and thee and thy seed after thee in their generations for an everlasting covenant, to be a God unto thee, and to thy seed after thee. And I will give unto thee, and to thy seed after thee, the land wherein thou art a stranger, all the land of Canaan, for an everlasting possession; and I will be their God.'

33 Acts 1.6: 'When they therefore were come together, they asked of him, saying, Lord, wilt thou at this time restore again the kingdom to Israel?'

34 1 Chronicles 17.14: 'But I will settle him in mine house and in my kingdom for ever: and his throne shall be established for evermore';

THE KINGDOM OF GOD IN THE PAST

LORD'S[35.] God has not forgotten His people Israel today. Although there came a time when God judicially judged Israel for rejecting their Messiah (*'blindness in part happened unto Israel'*[36]), this judgment will only continue until the *'Deliverer'* comes, which is a reference to the coming again of Christ. Then *'all Israel shall be saved'*. *'Thy kingdom come,'* was what the Saviour taught the disciples to pray – and come it will.

Past phase – when the Lord Jesus was on earth

The Lord Jesus, however, also spoke of the phase of the Kingdom of God from the days of John the Baptist unto His own day on earth, as being marked by persecution and violence[37]. The Lord Jesus had already shown in His famous "Sermon on the Mount" that His Kingdom has a present and spiritual reality now,[38] by using the present tense *'is'* when describing the Kingdom – *'theirs **is** the kingdom of Heaven'*. The Lord did not use a future tense i.e. not 'theirs shall be the Kingdom of Heaven'.

At this point Rome was dominating Israel. The Lord Jesus said concerning Himself as the King, *'The kingdom of God is come unto you'*[39] indicating a present meaning to the Kingdom when He was here on earth. This was not a mere foreshadowing of a future manifestation but a present reality – the King was in their midst. He said He was born King unlike all other kings: *'I am a king. To this end was I born'*[40], and that His Kingdom did not

---

Ex. 19.6: 'And ye shall be unto me a kingdom of priests, and an holy nation. These are the words which thou shalt speak unto the children of Israel.'

35 Psalm 22.28: 'For the kingdom is the LORD'S: and he is the governor among the nations.'

36 Rom. 11.25-26: 'For I would not, brethren, that ye should be ignorant of this mystery, lest ye should be wise in your own conceits; that blindness in part is happened to Israel, until the fulness of the Gentiles be come in. And so all Israel shall be saved: as it is written, There shall come out of Sion the Deliverer, and shall turn away ungodliness from Jacob.'

37 Matt. 11.12: 'And from the days of John the Baptist until now the kingdom of heaven suffereth violence.'

38 Matt. 5.3,10 - note the present tense "is"; (c.f. Matt.16.19; Jn. 18.36)

39 Matt. 12.28

40 John 18.37: 'I am a king. To this end was I born, and for this cause came I into the world, that I should bear witness unto the truth. Every one that is of the truth heareth my voice.'

THE EIGHT KINGDOM PARABLES

originate from this world.[41] Howbeit, many missed or rejected His claim to be King. The King's glory was veiled in humanity and the Kingdom of God was hidden and revealed by faith.

The Lord Jesus warned Israel that *'the kingdom of God shall be taken from you'*[42]. He also spoke about the Kingdom of God in a *mystery*[43]. We will seek to explain these aspects of the Kingdom in future chapters.

My Notes

---

41 John 18.36: 'My kingdom is not of this world: if my kingdom were of this world, then would my servants fight, that I should not be delivered to the Jews: but now is my kingdom not from hence.'

42 Matt. 21.43

43 Matt. 13.11: 'He answered and said unto them, Because it is given unto you to know the mysteries of the kingdom of heaven, but to them it is not given.';

Mark 4.11: 'And he said unto them, Unto you it is given to know the mystery of the kingdom of God: but unto them that are without, all these things are done in parables';

Luke 8.10: 'And he said, Unto you it is given to know the mysteries of the kingdom of God: but to others in parables; that seeing they might not see, and hearing they might not understand.'

THE KINGDOM OF GOD IN THE PAST

My Notes

What does Israel mean to God?

Chapter 3

THE KINGDOM OF GOD IN THE FUTURE

Enoch prophesied: *'the Lord cometh with ten thousands of his saints'*[44]. Abraham, too, looked forward to a golden age of blessing: he *'looked for a city which hath foundations, whose builder and maker is God'*[45]. He represented a group of Old Testament saints who *'desire a better country, that is, an heavenly: wherefore God is not ashamed to be called their God: for he hath prepared for them a city'*[46]. The prophets yearned for it;[47] the psalmist sang of it.[48] The Lord Jesus taught the disciples to pray about it, saying: *'Thy kingdom come'*[49]. He also taught His disciples that, although it was not in their power to identify when His Kingdom would come, He assured them implicitly that His Kingdom will come and that it is all in His Father's hand[50]. Most references, therefore, to the 'Kingdom'

---

44 Jude 14: 'And Enoch also, the seventh from Adam, prophesied of these, saying, Behold, the Lord cometh with ten thousands of his saints.'
45 Heb. 11.10 **46** Heb. 11.16
47 Isa. 32.1: 'Behold, a king shall reign in righteousness, and princes shall rule in judgment.'
48 Psalm 72.7-8: 'In his days shall the righteous flourish; and abundance of peace so long as the moon endureth. He shall have dominion also from sea to sea, and from the river unto the ends of the earth.'
49 Matt. 6.10
50 Acts 1.6-7: 'When they therefore were come together, they asked of him, saying, Lord, wilt thou at this time restore again the kingdom to Israel? And he said unto them, It is not for you to know the times or the seasons, which the Father hath put in his own power.'

THE EIGHT KINGDOM PARABLES

in Scripture concern that future Kingdom of God, pointing forward to when the Kingdom will have a physical reality[51] and Christ shall reign over this earth[52]. It will be then that God's desire to see Israel as a *Kingdom of priests* will be fully realised[53]. In the past, His sovereign rule would be seen in Israel. In this future, literal Kingdom on earth Christ will reign. The future Kingdom of Christ will *have no end*[54] and can never be defeated[55]

Jerusalem will be the capital of the world, called *Jehovah Shammah*[56], and be the epicentre of a rejuvenated world. One day the Kingdom will literally stretch from *sea to sea and from the river to the ends of the earth*[57]. What a day that will be! The truth of a future coming Kingdom, where the Lord Jesus will reign for one thousand years, is being marginalised today, but it is clearly taught in Scripture.

---

51 Matt. 6.10: 'Thy kingdom come. Thy will be done in earth, as it is in heaven'; Luke 22.30: 'That ye may eat and drink at my table in my kingdom, and sit on thrones, judging the twelve tribes of Israel.'

52 Zech.14.2-9: 'For I will gather all nations against Jerusalem to battle; and the city shall be taken, and the houses rifled, and the women ravished; and half of the city shall go forth into captivity, and the residue of the people shall not be cut off from the city. Then shall the LORD go forth, and fight against those nations, as when he fought in the day of battle. And his feet shall stand in that day upon the mount of Olives, which is before Jerusalem on the east, and the mount of Olives shall cleave in the midst thereof toward the east and toward the west, and there shall be a very great valley; and half of the mountain shall remove toward the north, and half of it toward the south. And ye shall flee to the valley of the mountains; for the valley of the mountains shall reach unto Azal: yea, ye shall flee, like as ye fled from before the earthquake in the days of Uzziah king of Judah: and the LORD my God shall come, and all the saints with thee. And it shall come to pass in that day, that the light shall not be clear, nor dark: But it shall be one day which shall be known to the LORD, not day, nor night: but it shall come to pass, that at evening time it shall be light. And it shall be in that day, that living waters shall go out from Jerusalem; half of them toward the former sea, and half of them toward the hinder sea: in summer and in winter shall it be. And the LORD shall be king over all the earth: in that day shall there be one LORD, and his name one.'

53 Ex. 19.6: 'And ye shall be unto me a kingdom of priests, and an holy nation. These are the words which thou shalt speak unto the children of Israel.'

54 Isa. 9.7: 'Of the increase of his government and peace there shall be no end, upon the throne of David, and upon his kingdom, to order it, and to establish it with judgment and with justice from henceforth even for ever. The zeal of the LORD of hosts will perform this.'

THE KINGDOM OF GOD IN THE FUTURE

In Revelation 20, the one-thousand-year (Millennium) period of the reign of Christ is mentioned six times: '*and they lived and reigned with Christ a thousand years*'[58]. The Millennium will commence after the Lord returns in judgment on the earth (Revelation 19).

What are the reasons for the Millennium?

(1) God's covenant promise to Abraham[59] and David[60] that their offspring would inhabit Emmanuel's Land.

(2) God's answer to the prayer of the remnant: '*Thy kingdom come*'[61].

(3) God's final test for man. Despite the most ideal of circumstances and with Satan locked up for one thousand years[62] and in no way able to influence matters on earth, the human race will still fail and it will prove that the '*carnal mind is enmity against God*'[63].

---

55 Dan. 2.44: 'And in the days of these kings shall the God of heaven set up a Kingdom, which shall never be destroyed: and the kingdom shall not be left to other people, but it shall break in pieces and consume all these kingdoms, and it shall stand for ever.'

56 Ezek. 48.35: 'It was round about eighteen thousand measures: and the name of the city from that day shall be, The LORD is there (Jehovah Shammah).'

57 Psalm 72.8: 'He shall have dominion also from sea to sea, and from the river unto the ends of the earth.'

58 Rev 20.1-7 'And I saw an angel come down from heaven, having the key of the bottomless pit and a great chain in his hand. And he laid hold on the dragon, that old serpent, which is the Devil, and Satan, and bound him a thousand years, And cast him into the bottomless pit, and shut him up, and set a seal upon him, that he should deceive the nations no more, till the thousand years should be fulfilled: and after that he must be loosed a little season. And I saw thrones, and they sat upon them, and judgment was given unto them: and I saw the souls of them that were beheaded for the witness of Jesus, and for the word of God, and which had not worshipped the beast, neither his image, neither had received his mark upon their foreheads, or in their hands; and they lived and reigned with Christ a thousand years. But the rest of the dead lived not again until the thousand years were finished. This is the first resurrection. Blessed and holy is he that hath part in the first resurrection: on such the second death hath no power, but they shall be priests of God and of Christ, and shall reign with him a thousand years. And when the thousand years are expired, Satan shall be loosed out of his prison,'

59 Gen. 17.7-8: 'And I will establish my covenant between me and thee and thy seed after thee in their generations for an everlasting covenant, to be a God unto thee, and to thy seed after thee. And I will give unto thee, and to thy seed after thee, the land wherein thou art a stranger, all the land of Canaan, for an everlasting possession; and I will be their God.'

THE EIGHT KINGDOM PARABLES

What will the Millennium be like?

(1) A Time of Refreshing for Israel

*'Repent ye therefore, and be converted, that your sins may be blotted out, when **the times of refreshing** shall come from the presence of the Lord'*[64].

(2) A Time of Righteousness for the World

*'Behold, a king shall **reign in righteousness**, and princes shall rule in judgment. And a man shall be as an hiding place from the wind, and a covert from the tempest; as rivers of water in a dry place, as the shadow of a great rock in a weary land';*[65]

*'Because he hath appointed a day, in the which he will **judge the world in righteousness** by that man whom he hath ordained; whereof he hath given assurance unto all men, in that he hath raised him from the dead.'*[66]

(3) A Time of Rule for Christ

*'Behold, the days come, saith the LORD, that I will raise unto David a righteous Branch, **and a King shall reign** and prosper, and shall execute judgment and justice in the earth. In his days Judah shall be saved, and Israel shall dwell safely: and this is his name whereby he shall be called, THE LORD OUR RIGHTEOUSNESS'*[67].

(4) A Time of Rest and Prosperity for all Nations

'And he shall judge among many people, and rebuke strong nations afar off; and they shall beat their swords into plowshares, and their spears into

---

60 2 Sam. 7.12-16: ' And when thy days be fulfilled, and thou shalt sleep with thy fathers, I will set up thy seed after thee, which shall proceed out of thy bowels, and I will establish his kingdom. He shall build an house for my name, and I will stablish the throne of his kingdom for ever. I will be his father, and he shall be my son. If he commit iniquity, I will chasten him with the rod of men, and with the stripes of the children of men: But my mercy shall not depart away from him, as I took it from Saul, whom I put away before thee. And thine house and thy kingdom shall be established for ever before thee: thy throne shall be established for ever.'

THE KINGDOM OF GOD IN THE FUTURE

> ❝❝ *Satan will be placed in the bottomless pit for the 1000 years of Christ's Millennial reign*

pruninghooks: nation shall not lift up a sword against nation, neither shall they learn war anymore[68].

Appendix 1 lists seven transforming features that will take place in the Millennial Kingdom. The world will return to Eden conditions, poverty will be put away forever, righteousness will rule, harmony will be at home and peace will flow like a river in this world. Hallelujah!

Who will populate the Millennium?

(1) Saved Gentiles who have believed the Gospel of the Kingdom during the Tribulation[69].

(2) Saved Jews in the Tribulation including 144000 Jewish men active in the Tribulation period[70].

(3) Resurrected Old Testament saints including Abraham, Isaac and Jacob[71]. The resurrection is predicted in Old Testament[72]. All who enter will be saved.

What about Satan?

Satan will be placed in the bottomless pit for the 1000 years of Christ's Millennial reign[73]. He will be unable to interfere with the world at that time. Despite the utopian conditions, however, a people will rise up in rebellion against Christ.

---

61 Matt. 6.10 **62** Rev. 20.1-3 **63** Rom. 8.7 **64** Acts 3.19
65 Isa. 32.1 **66** Acts 17.31 **67** Jer. 23.5-6 **68** Micah 4.3
69 Rev. 7.9-17 **70** Rev. 7.5-8
71 Matt. 8.11: 'And I say unto you, That many shall come from the east and west, and shall sit down with Abraham, and Isaac, and Jacob, in the kingdom of heaven.'
72 Daniel 12.2: 'And many of them that sleep in the dust of the earth shall awake, some to everlasting life, and some to shame and everlasting contempt.'
73 Rev. 20.2-3

THE EIGHT KINGDOM PARABLES

What about Israel?

The true Israel shall be saved for ever: '*But Israel shall be saved in the LORD with an everlasting salvation: ye shall not be ashamed nor confounded world without end*'[74].

Israel shall be blessed eternally: '*Thy sun shall no more go down; neither shall thy moon withdraw itself: for the LORD shall be thine everlasting light, and the days of thy mourning shall be ended*'[75].

What is the secret of the peace in the Millennium?

The name of God will be feared, and the will of God will be the controlling force for the thousand-year reign[76].

What will be the relationship of the Church to the Millennial Kingdom?

We must leave this subject to a future chapter, but in Revelation 21 we read of the 'New Jerusalem'[77] descending out from Heaven. We never read of it touching the earth, however, and we read that Millennial people will walk in the light of that city[78]. If this cubic or pyramidic city, with dimensions of 1500 miles cubed,[79] is placed physically on the earth in approximately the area where Jerusalem currently is, then we have a contradiction with

---

74 Isa. 45.17 **75** Isa. 60.20

76 Zech. 14.9: 'And the LORD shall be king over all the earth: in that day shall there be one LORD, and his name one';

Isa. 66.12: 'For thus saith the LORD, Behold, I will extend peace to her like a river, and the glory of the Gentiles like a flowing stream: then shall ye suck, ye shall be borne upon her sides, and be dandled upon her knees.'

77 Rev. 21.2: 'And I John saw the holy city, new Jerusalem, coming down from God out of heaven, prepared as a bride adorned for her husband.'

78 Rev. 21.24: 'And the nations of them which are saved shall walk in the light of it: and the kings of the earth do bring their glory and honour into it.'

79 Rev 21.16: 'And the city lieth foursquare, and the length is as large as the breadth: and he measured the city with the reed, twelve thousand furlongs. The length and the breadth and the height of it are equal.'

THE KINGDOM OF GOD IN THE FUTURE

Zechariah 14[80]. This passage describes a plateau on which the earthly Jerusalem in the Millennial Kingdom sits. The plateau is just over 40 miles long from Geba (6 miles North of Jerusalem) to Rimmon (35 miles south of Jerusalem). It then gives specific details of certain parts of the city to show how literal this city is, including the corner gate and the tower of Hananeel in the North East corner of the city. This literal city in the Millennium is reinforced in the prophecy of Jeremiah 31[81]. The changed topography of Jerusalem, when the Lord returns, is described in detail in Zechariah 14 and it cannot be squared with a belief that the heavenly city of 1500 miles square descends and remains upon the earth in this location, nor is it consistent with the description of the temple in Ezekiel 40-48 which is physically upon the earth in the Millennium. If the Holy City coming out from heaven in Revelation 21 is above the earth, then both passages (Rev. 21 and Zech. 14) can be understood and there is no contradiction. This distinction between the earthly and heavenly Jerusalem seems to be suggesting that there is a distinction between God's earthly people and God's heavenly people in the Millennial Kingdom. However, as we shall show in a subsequent chapter, and in the appendix, the Church which must be resident in this city shall be the administration centre of the Kingdom and roles and responsibilities will be given to the Church over the Kingdom. We shall have bodies that are not limited by time and space and '*ascending and descending*' shall take place, and full harmony will exist between heaven and earth[82]. The barriers to travel we

---

80 Zech. 14.10-11: 'All the land shall be turned as a plain from Geba to Rimmon south of Jerusalem: and it shall be lifted up, and inhabited in her place, from Benjamin's gate unto the place of the first gate, unto the corner gate, and from the tower of Hananeel unto the king's winepresses. And men shall dwell in it, and there shall be no more utter destruction; but Jerusalem shall be safely inhabited.'

81 Jer. 31.38-40: 'Behold, the days come, saith the LORD, that the city shall be built to the LORD from the tower of Hananeel unto the gate of the corner. And the measuring line shall yet go forth over against it upon the hill Gareb, and shall compass about to Goath. And the whole valley of the dead bodies, and of the ashes, and all the fields unto the brook of Kidron, unto the corner of the horse gate toward the east, shall be holy unto the LORD; it shall not be plucked up, nor thrown down any more for ever.'

82 John 1.51: 'And he saith unto him, Verily, verily, I say unto you, Hereafter ye shall see heaven open, and the angels of God ascending and descending upon the Son of man.'

THE EIGHT KINGDOM PARABLES

experience today will no longer be a difficulty – remember how the Lord Jesus appeared in the Upper Room in His resurrected body despite the doors being locked[83]. The Church will be part and parcel of the Kingdom, although always distinct from Israel.

Is the Millennial Kingdom the final phase of the Kingdom?

No! Although Israel as a nation will never apostatise once they have accepted their Messiah, individual children born into saved families will still have the propensity to sin and it is they who will join the army of Satan, at his release after a thousand years. People born in the Millennium will need salvation, proving that sin is an innate part of human nature and not the effect of adverse circumstances. In summary:

(1)   The Millennium is not the Eternal State, as death is not destroyed nor Satan[84]. Isaiah 35 also tells us that the Lord will perform miracles of healing in the Millennium Kingdom[85].

(2)   The Millennium is not the Eternal State, as declension is apparent, and discontentment grows[86]. The Devil will find a spirit of discontent amongst some, that he can galvanize when he is released.

83 John 20.26: 'And after eight days again his disciples were within, and Thomas with them: then came Jesus, the doors being shut, and stood in the midst, and said, Peace be unto you.'

84 1 Cor. 15.24-26: 'Then cometh the end, when he shall have delivered up the kingdom to God, even the Father; when he shall have put down all rule and all authority and power. For he must reign, till he hath put all enemies under his feet. The last enemy that shall be destroyed is death.'

85 Isa. 35.5-6

86 Rev. 20.8: 'And shall go out to deceive the nations which are in the four quarters of the earth, Gog and Magog, to gather them together to battle: the number of whom is as the sand of the sea.' This decline is hinted at in the feast of tabernacles, always associated with the kingdom, where a gradual decline in the appreciation of Christ is seen in a gradual decrease in the number of bullocks offered (Num. 29. 12-38).

87 Zech. 14.16-19: 'And it shall come to pass, that every one that is left of all the nations which came against Jerusalem shall even go up from year to year to worship the King, the LORD of hosts, and to keep the feast of tabernacles. And it shall be, that whoso will not come up of all the families of the earth unto Jerusalem to worship the King,

THE KINGDOM OF GOD IN THE FUTURE

> ❝ *The Millennium is not the Eternal State, as there is need for discipline in the Millennium*

(3) The Millennium is not the Eternal State, as there is need for discipline in the Millennium. The Gentiles, for example, are required to keep the Feast of Tabernacles and to send representatives to Jerusalem. But God will chasten Egypt and other nations by withholding rain when they fail to comply with this command of the Lord[87]. We also know that capital punishment will be inflicted[88].

How can such a large army be gathered against the Lord at the end of the 1000 years?

(1) Death will be the exception in the Millennium, therefore there will be a massive population expansion[89]. A person that dies at a hundred will be regarded to be a child.

(2) The Devil will quickly resume his devilish practices[90].

(3) The human race is depraved and, given the opportunity, they will sin[91].

---

the LORD of hosts, even upon them shall be no rain. And if the family of Egypt go not up, and come not, that have no rain; there shall be the plague, wherewith the LORD will smite the heathen that come not up to keep the feast of tabernacles. This shall be the punishment of Egypt, and the punishment of all nations that come not up to keep the feast of tabernacles.

88 Isa. 11.4 'But with righteousness shall he judge the poor, and reprove with equity for the meek of the earth: and he shall smite the earth with the rod of his mouth, and with the breath of his lips shall he slay the wicked.'

89 Isa. 65.20: 'There shall be no more thence an infant of days, nor an old man that hath not filled his days: for the child shall die an hundred years old; but the sinner being an hundred years old shall be accursed.'

90 Rev. 20.7-8: 'And when the thousand years are expired, Satan shall be loosed out of his prison, And shall go out to deceive the nations which are in the four quarters of the earth, Gog and Magog, to gather them together to battle: the number of whom is as the sand of the sea.'

91 Jer. 17.9: 'The heart is deceitful above all things, and desperately wicked: who can know it?'

THE EIGHT KINGDOM PARABLES

Ultimate and eternal phase of the Kingdom

Paul spoke of the ultimate phase of the Kingdom being a *'heavenly kingdom'*[92], which at the very least includes heaven, where the Lord Jesus is just now, but also looks even further ahead. John saw an eternal state of perfection which he records for us as he describes the holy city and a new heaven and a new earth in the final chapters of Revelation. Peter saw a final perfect eternal state which he calls the *day of God*, recording it for us in the final chapter of his second epistle[93].

So, the universal Kingdom truth is progressively revealed by faith, with a past phase in Israel, a future phase when the Lord comes to reign on earth for a thousand years, and a final phase in the eternal state. What about the Kingdom of God in the present when Israel is rejecting their Messiah? This is the subject of the next chapter.

My Notes

---

92 2 Tim. 4.18: 'And the Lord shall deliver me from every evil work, and will preserve me unto his heavenly kingdom: to whom be glory for ever and ever. Amen.'
93 2 Peter 3.12-13: 'Looking for and hasting unto the coming of the day of God, wherein the heavens being on fire shall be dissolved, and the elements shall melt with fervent heat? Nevertheless we, according to his promise, look for new heavens and a new earth, wherein dwelleth righteousness.'

THE KINGDOM OF GOD IN THE FUTURE

My Notes

What are the key features of the future Kingdom of God on earth?

Chapter 4

THE KINGDOM IN MYSTERY IN THE PRESENT

Present Phase

We have seen past and future and ultimate eternal phases of the Kingdom of God. What about the Kingdom of God now? As indicated earlier, the Lord Jesus used the present tense of the Kingdom of God in His first beatitude in the Sermon on the Mount[94]. He spoke of a day when He would leave this world and of a day when He would return. He warned Israel that the *'kingdom of God would be taken from'* them and *'given to a nation bringing forth the fruits.'*[95] This *nation* would include Gentile people who would come into the good of the Kingdom. This age would be between the rejection of Christ by Israel and His return in glory as King. This inter-advent period includes the *Church* period phase of the Kingdom, and the period just prior to the advent of Christ after the Church has been raptured to heaven, called the *Tribulation* period of the Kingdom, so that, although the Church is not the Kingdom, it is part of the Kingdom. The Church was a new organism introduced by the Lord in Matthew 16, and carried the thought of a future reality: *'I will build my Church'*. He was not referring to Israel, as Israel had already been in place for thousands of

---

94 Matt. 5.3: 'Blessed are the poor in spirit: for theirs is the kingdom of heaven.'
95 Matt. 21.43: 'Therefore say I unto you, The kingdom of God shall be taken from you, and given to a nation bringing forth the fruits thereof.'

THE EIGHT KINGDOM PARABLES

years. This Church is a mystery that Paul unfolds in the Ephesian epistle[96]; Israel was not a mystery. (This is one of the reasons why the Lord refers to the *Kingdom of God presently* as hidden, in a mystery, which we will discuss shortly.)[97] The Church is new: '*one new man*' incorporating Jew and Gentile[98]; Israel was not new.

The language used of the Church is the language of the Kingdom. The Lord introduced the term 'Church' (*ekklesia* – a gathered out company) in the same breath as using the word 'Kingdom' (*basileia*). He said to Peter '... *upon this rock I will build my* **Church***; and the gates of hell shall not prevail against it. And I will give unto thee* [Peter] *the keys of the* **kingdom of heaven***: and whatsoever thou shalt bind on earth shall be bound in heaven: and whatsoever thou shalt loose on earth shall be loosed in heaven*'[99]. Peter clearly had a role in the progressive development of the Kingdom in the Church period, opening the door with the *keys of the Kingdom,* to Jews (Acts 2) and Gentiles (Acts 10).

Therefore, the Church perfected is the total of all who in all places and times have accepted Christ as their Lord[100] and have been translated out of the authority of darkness into the authority and kingdom of the Son of God's love. Paul, by the Spirit, tells us that upon our salvation - God: '*delivered us from the power of darkness, and hath translated us into the kingdom of his dear Son*'[101]. Every true believer in the Lord Jesus, from Pentecost to the Lord's return

---

96 Eph. 3.9: 'And to make all men see what is the fellowship of the mystery, which from the beginning of the world hath been hid in God, who created all things by Jesus Christ';
Eph. 5. 32: 'This is a great mystery: but I speak concerning Christ and the church.'
97 Matt. 13.11: 'He answered and said unto them, Because it is given unto you to know the mysteries of the kingdom of heaven, but to them it is not given.'
98 Eph. 2.15: 'Having abolished in his flesh the enmity, even the law of commandments contained in ordinances; for to make in himself of twain one new man, so making peace'.
99 Matt. 16.18-19
100 1 Cor. 12.3: 'Wherefore I give you to understand, that no man speaking by the Spirit of God calleth Jesus accursed: and that no man can say that Jesus is the Lord, but by the Holy Ghost.'
101 Col. 1.13 **102** Matt. 18.17-20

THE KINGDOM IN MYSTERY IN THE PRESENT

> ❝ *The Church is...the official administration of the coming kingdom of God in the Holy city...*

to the air, is in both the Church which is His body and the Kingdom of the Son of His love.

The 'Kingdom' language is also employed in Scripture of the local assembly. The Lord Jesus also taught the truth about the local Church in Matthew 18, where, in a locality, believers would gather to the Name of the Lord Jesus, taking no sectarian title[102]. Today, in the present phase of the Kingdom, in the Church period, His *Kingdom* authority and *power* would be seen in the assembly of God's people in each locality[103] where believers gather to the Name of the Lord Jesus alone with no other supra-authority than the Lord Jesus Christ. When authority was required in the assembly for discipline, the assembly was likened to a Kingdom[104], in the context of reminding us that in a future Kingdom we shall *'judge the world'*[105]. The Church is therefore the ruling body, the official administration of the coming Kingdom of God in the holy city, with saints having roles over the earth and sitting on thrones[106]. This is why the Saviour said to His disciples: *'Fear not, little flock; for it is your Father's good pleasure to give you the Kingdom'*[107], and promised the assembly in Thyatira that they would have *power over the nations*[108]. Paul also exhorts the Jewish

---

103 1 Cor. 4.18-21: 'Now some are puffed up, as though I would not come to you. But I will come to you shortly, if the Lord will, and will know, not the speech of them which are puffed up, but the power. For the kingdom of God is not in word, but in power. What will ye? shall I come unto you with a rod, or in love, and in the spirit of meekness?'
104 1 Cor. 6.9: 'Know ye not that the unrighteous shall not inherit the kingdom of God?'; 1 Cor. 5.4-5: 'In the name of our Lord Jesus Christ, when ye are gathered together, and my spirit, with the power of our Lord Jesus Christ, To deliver such an one unto Satan for the destruction of the flesh, that the spirit may be saved in the day of the Lord Jesus.'
105 1 Cor. 6.2-3
106 Rev. 3.21: 'To him that overcometh will I grant to sit with me in my throne, even as I also overcame, and am set down with my Father in his throne.'
107 Luke 12.32 **108** Rev. 2.26

THE EIGHT KINGDOM PARABLES

and Gentile members of the assembly in Rome to display the 'Kingdom features' of peace and joy now, instead of arguing over food: *'For the Kingdom of God is not meat and drink; but righteousness, and peace, and joy in the Holy Ghost'*[109]. We are now *'ambassadors'* for that Kingdom[110], *citizens* of a heavenly Kingdom[111] and part of a *kingly priesthood*[112]. We are royalty – what a thought! Let us behave in keeping with our calling. We who *'preach the kingdom of God'*, like Paul[113], must realise we preach the present and final fulfilment of this Kingdom. It is only in this way that we can understand that we are *'fellow-workers unto the kingdom of God'*[114].

Why are the parables a mystery?

The Lord Jesus said that the Kingdom parables were the *'mysteries of the kingdom of heaven'* which *'was given'* to them (i.e. the disciples) *'to know'*[115]. Mysteries in Scripture are no longer mysterious but are truths heretofore unrevealed but now revealed by faith. A good definition of a biblical mystery is given by Paul to the Colossians[116]: *'Even the mystery which hath been hid from ages and from generations, but now is made manifest to his saints'*. The truth of the Kingdom coming, a literal Kingdom where the Messiah would reign, had already been taught in the Old Testament Scriptures. That was not a mystery. It must be, therefore, the present manifestation of this Kingdom in the inter-advent period, which includes, although is not synonymous with, the Church age. This is the 'mystery' truth of the Kingdom that is being more fully revealed in these parables. Therefore, Matthew records: *'I will utter things which have been kept secret from the foundation of the world'*[117]. It is interesting that it is in Matthew uniquely that the Kingdom Parables are revealed, in chapter 13, and the Church is uniquely revealed in chapter 16[118],

---

109 Rom. 14.17

110 2 Cor. 5.20: 'Now then we are ambassadors for Christ, as though God did beseech you by us: we pray you in Christ's stead, be ye reconciled to God.'

111 Phil. 3.20: 'For our conversation [citizenship] is in heaven; from whence also we look for the Saviour, the Lord Jesus Christ.'

112 1 Pet. 2.9: 'But ye are a chosen generation, a royal priesthood, an holy nation, a peculiar people; that ye should shew forth the praises of him who hath called you out of darkness into his marvellous light.'

113 Acts 20.25: 'And now, behold, I know that ye all, among whom I have gone preaching the kingdom of God, shall see my face no more.'

THE KINGDOM IN MYSTERY IN THE PRESENT

and then the local Church is uniquely revealed in chapter 18[119] all by the Lord Jesus. This is by design. Also, chapter 12 ends with the Lord explaining that the true relationships are spiritual and not natural: *'For whosoever shall do the will of my Father which is in heaven, the same is my brother, and sister, and mother'*[120]. Chapter 13 commences by focussing on the idea of a spiritual relationship in the Kingdom. We should therefore perhaps expect to see some of this 'hidden spiritual truth' of the present phase of the Kingdom of God to be developed in these 'Kingdom Parables', even although the ultimate fulfilment is the future literal Kingdom on earth.

A cartesian diagram sometimes helps to explain complex ideas. This diagram will show what the Kingdom of God involves. The big circle is the Kingdom of God and includes smaller circles like Israel, the Church, saints saved during the Tribulation after the Lord has come for His people but before He judges the world, and a Millennial Kingdom, consisting of restored Israel and Gentile nations.

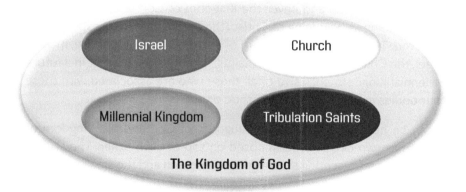

114 Col. 4.11 115 Matt. 13.11 116 Col. 1.26 117 Matt. 13.34-35

118 Matt. 16.18-19: 'And I say also unto thee, that thou art Peter, and upon this rock I will build my church; and the gates of hell shall not prevail against it. And I will give unto thee the keys of the kingdom of heaven: and whatsoever thou shalt bind on earth shall be bound in heaven: and whatsoever thou shalt loose on earth shall be loosed in heaven.'

119 Matt. 18.17: 'And if he shall neglect to hear them, tell it unto the church: but if he neglect to hear the church, let him be unto thee as an heathen man and a publican.'

120 Matt. 12.50

What is the difference between the Kingdom of God and the Kingdom of Heaven?

In describing some of these parables both Mark and Luke speak of the Kingdom of God whereas Matthew normally speaks of the Kingdom of Heaven. For the avoidance of any doubt, there is only one Kingdom – not two! However, for those interested there is a subtle difference between the Kingdom of God and the Kingdom of Heaven, and this is discussed more fully in appendix 1. The expression the 'Kingdom of God' seems to include only those who are truly born again (John 3. 3, 7) – so only the authentic within the Old Testament saints, Church, Tribulation saints and the restored Israel in a future day are contained within this title. The expression 'Kingdom of Heaven' includes all who are born again but also carries with it the wider thought of profession: that is, it includes those who claim to belong to the King (but some are false) throughout all ages. This is why the parable of the Wheat and Tares[121] is likened unto the Kingdom of Heaven and never the Kingdom of God: it contains people masquerading as belonging to Christ (the tares), only to be exposed and removed. The expression 'Kingdom of Heaven' would, therefore, include Israel, the Church, the Tribulation saints, and the rule of Christ in a future Millennial Kingdom inclusive of all those who are associated with these four bodies as well, whether authentic or not.

It can be helpful to think of the Kingdom of God and the Kingdom of Heaven as two circles superimposed on top of each other. The slightly larger circle representing the Kingdom of Heaven and the smaller one the Kingdom of God.

The Kingdom of God and the Kingdom of Heaven

121 Matt. 13. 24-30

THE KINGDOM IN MYSTERY IN THE PRESENT

My Notes

What are the features of the present phase of the kingdom?

___
___
___
___
___
___
___
___
___

Chapter 5

THE KINGDOM OF GOD IN THE TRIBULATION

The present phase of the Kingdom in mystery, the inter-advent period of the Messiah, will soon come to an end. The first sign that it will soon end is the first stage of the return of the Lord Jesus, which will be to the air for the Church. The 'Church Age' which has known the descent of the Spirit of God, the preaching of the Gospel of the Grace of God and much more, now awaits the soon return of the Lord Jesus. There are many differences between the coming of the Lord Jesus to the air for His people and His coming to Earth to reign with His people. It is one coming but in two stages. His coming to earth to be Saviour was in two stages. The first stage was to rural Bethlehem away from the public gaze, and then the second stage was a public appearing in Jerusalem as Messiah, riding on the back of a donkey[122]. His second coming will be no different – it will be in two stages. The first stage will be *to the air* privately for His people[123]; the second stage will be publicly *to the earth* in judgment to reign in His Kingdom[124].

---

122 Matt. 21.1-16
123 1 Thess. 4.17: 'Then we which are alive and remain shall be caught up together with them in the clouds, to meet the Lord in the air: and so shall we ever be with the Lord.'
124 Zech. 14.4 : 'And his feet shall stand in that day upon the mount of Olives, which is before Jerusalem on the east, and the mount of Olives shall cleave in the midst thereof toward the east and toward the west, and there shall be a very great valley; and half of the mountain shall remove toward the north, and half of it toward the south';

THE EIGHT KINGDOM PARABLES

The second stage of the Lord's second coming to reign as King on earth was mentioned often in the Old Testament, but not the first stage – what we call the Rapture, the Lord's return to the air. Paul defends the resurrection from the Old Testament Scriptures in 1 Corinthians 15, but he does not do this when describing events surrounding the Rapture. This was a new revelation (called a 'mystery') for the Church[125] and Paul commences discussing the Rapture by saying, *'by the word of the Lord'*[126] – in other words the truth of the first stage of the Lord's second coming for the Church was truth uniquely revealed in the New Testament alone.

What does the word Rapture mean?

The word rapture means *'caught up'*[127] and has the idea of a 'snatching' or 'catching' away. It was used in Greek literature to describe a mother 'snatching' her child from danger or of a thief 'snatching' his booty quickly. So, the Lord will catch away His people suddenly and silently from this world. The law of gravitation will be offset – *'caught UP'* and the law of decomposition will be offset - *'dead in Christ shall rise first'*.

Will the Rapture be only for the Church?

Yes. The fourth chapter of 1 Thessalonians is a passage that emphasises the Lordship of Christ, and yet it is interesting to note the one verse where there is an exception is the verse that describes who will be

---

2 Thess. 1.7-8: 'And to you who are troubled rest with us, when the Lord Jesus shall be revealed from heaven with his mighty angels, In flaming fire taking vengeance on them that know not God, and that obey not the gospel of our Lord Jesus Christ.'

125 1 Cor. 15.51: 'Behold, I shew you a mystery; We shall not all sleep, but we shall all be changed.'

126 1 Thess. 4.15: 'For this we say unto you by the word of the Lord, that we which are alive and remain unto the coming of the Lord shall not prevent them which are asleep.'

127 1 Thess. 4.17

128 1 Thess. 4.16: 'For the Lord himself shall descend from heaven with a shout, with the voice of the archangel, and with the trump of God: and the dead in Christ shall rise first.'

129 Heb. 11.13: 'These all died in faith, not having received the promises, but having seen them afar off ...'

130 1 Cor. 15. 51

THE KINGDOM OF GOD IN THE TRIBULATION

resurrected and raptured. It does not say the 'dead in our Lord Jesus Christ' but *'the dead in Christ'*[128] i.e. all saved (in Christ) will rise to be with Him. The expression 'in Christ' appears 77 times in our Bible and on each occasion is unique to the Church. Israel are described as dying *'in faith'*[129] but never *'in Christ'*. Paul says to the Corinthians: *'We shall **all** be changed'*[130]. Our participation in the Rapture does not depend on how loyally we have acknowledged His Lordship but simply on the fact that we are in Christ. There is nothing 'partial' about the Rapture[131]. All the Church will go at the same time.

Why is the time of the Rapture withheld?

God knows that if we could predict the actual date of the Rapture or indeed anticipate pre-rapture signs, there would be that real danger that we could be occupied with the 'event' more than the 'Person of Christ'. It would also rob of us of 'urgency' in our Gospel witness and remove the need to be 'watchful' in personal holiness[132].

What happens after the Rapture?

Whilst there may be a transition period, the Bible speaks of a specific period of seven years of carnage and turmoil on earth prior to the time when the Lord comes back to the earth, the Tribulation[133] or Daniel's 70th week[134]. The longest descriptions of this period are found from Revelation chapter six through to Revelation chapter 19 but Matthew 24, Mark 13, and

---

131 Rom. 8.23: 'And not only they, but ourselves also, which have the firstfruits of the Spirit, even we ourselves groan within ourselves, waiting for the adoption, to wit, the redemption of our body.'

132 1 John 2.28: 'And now, little children, abide in him; that, when he shall appear, we may have confidence, and not be ashamed before him at his coming.'

133 Matt. 24.21: 'For then shall be great tribulation, such as was not since the beginning of the world to this time, no, nor ever shall be';

Matt. 24.29: 'Immediately after the tribulation of those days shall the sun be darkened, and the moon shall not give her light, and the stars shall fall from heaven, and the powers of the heavens shall be shaken.'

134 Dan. 9.27: 'And he shall confirm the covenant with many for one week (means in context a week of years): and in the midst of the week he shall cause the sacrifice and the oblation to cease, and for the overspreading of abominations he shall make it desolate, even until the consummation, and that determined shall be poured upon the desolate.'

THE EIGHT KINGDOM PARABLES

Luke 21 also provide extensive descriptions of this period, particularly the last part of this period. The last half of this seven-year period is called the 'great Tribulation'[135] and lasts 1260 days[136] or 42 months of thirty days[137] or 3.5 years[138]. The question might be asked: will the Church go through this period of Tribulation?

Will the Church go through the Tribulation?

The answer to this question is an emphatic 'No'. Appendix 2 will list seven reasons why the Church will not go through the Tribulation. At this stage we will just give three reasons:

(1) No, because the coming of Christ to the air was believed to be imminent

The early Christians did not anticipate going through a period of extensive world-wide judgment upon earth because they were expecting the return of Christ at any moment.

---

135 Matt. 24.21
136 Rev 12.6: 'And the woman fled into the wilderness, where she hath a place prepared of God, that they should feed her there a thousand two hundred and threescore days.'
137 Rev. 11.2: 'But the court which is without the temple leave out, and measure it not; for it is given unto the Gentiles: and the holy city shall they tread under foot forty and two months.'
138 Rev 12.14: 'And to the woman were given two wings of a great eagle, that she might fly into the wilderness, into her place, where she is nourished for a time, and times, and half a time, from the face of the serpent.' Time equals 1 year, times equals 2 years, and half a time equals half a year and so added together give 3.5 years.
139 John 14.1-3: 'Let not your heart be troubled: ye believe in God, believe also in me. In my Father's house are many mansions: if it were not so, I would have told you. I go to prepare a place for you. And if I go and prepare a place for you, I will come again, and receive you unto myself; that where I am, there ye may be also';
John 21.22-23; 'Jesus saith unto him, If I will that he tarry till I come, what is that to thee? follow thou me. 23Then went this saying abroad among the brethren, that that disciple should not die: yet Jesus said not unto him, He shall not die; but, If I will that he tarry till I come, what is that to thee?'
140 1 Cor. 16.22 141 Rev. 22.20
142 2 Cor. 5.1-2: 'For we know that if [please notice the 'if' – it was a possibility that their earthly house (their body) need not be dissolved or that they might not need

THE KINGDOM OF GOD IN THE TRIBULATION

- They took the words of Christ at face value[139].

- They greeted each other with '*Maranatha*' believing that His coming was soon[140]. John ends the Bible saying, '*Even so, come, Lord Jesus*'[141].

- They held out to one another the possibility of not dying[142]. Their core belief was, '*We shall not all sleep*'[143].

- They comforted each other with the thought of His imminent coming[144] saying, it was a '*little while*'[145].

- They regarded the first evidence of salvation to be people who were '*waiting for his Son from heaven*'[146].

(2) No, because the structure of the book of Revelation does not allow it

Revelation 6 to 18 is the Tribulation period and the Church is not mentioned once in this section, despite the fact that the book is written to the 7 Churches[147]. After chapter 3 we never read again of the Church until we see her coming out of heaven in chapter 19. In almost every

---

to be naked in death but clothed upon] our earthly house of this tabernacle were dissolved, we have a building of God, an house not made with hands, eternal in the heavens. ²For in this we groan, earnestly desiring to be clothed upon with our house which is from heaven:

143 1 Cor. 15.51: 'Behold, I shew you a mystery; We shall not all sleep, but we shall all be changed.'

144 1 Thess. 4.13-18: 'But I would not have you to be ignorant, brethren, concerning them which are asleep, that ye sorrow not, even as others which have no hope. For if we believe that Jesus died and rose again, even so them also which sleep in Jesus will God bring with him. For this we say unto you by the word of the Lord, that we which are alive and remain unto the coming of the Lord shall not prevent them which are asleep. For the Lord himself shall descend from heaven with a shout, with the voice of the archangel, and with the trump of God: and the dead in Christ shall rise first: Then we which are alive and remain shall be caught up together with them in the clouds, to meet the Lord in the air: and so shall we ever be with the Lord. Wherefore comfort one another with these words.'

145 Heb. 10.37: 'For yet a little while, and he that shall come will come, and will not tarry.'

146 1 Thess. 1.10

147 Rev. 1.4: 'John to the seven churches which are in Asia: Grace be unto you, and peace, from him which is, and which was, and which is to come; and from the seven Spirits which are before his throne'.

THE EIGHT KINGDOM PARABLES

chapter in this section (chapters 4 - 18) we can see things which would exclude us. Can we pray the prayer of Rev. 6. 10?[148] That prayer is not how our Lord prayed in Luke 23. 34![149] In Revelation 7 there are two groups of people, Jews and Gentiles, quite distinct, but in the Church, God has, *'made in himself of two one new man'*[150]. There are no such distinctions in the Church. Additionally, in Rev. 19. 1-10 the Church is in heaven before the return of Christ to earth. The Lord comes as King of Kings out of Heaven to reign from verse 11 onwards in this chapter[151]. But the Church (the Bride) is already in Heaven clothed in righteousness from verses 1-10. How did she get there? She was transported there beforehand[152]. When the world is cursing God for His judgments[153], the Church will be in heaven with Christ.

(3) No, because the New Testament explicitly teaches the reverse

To the Church at Philadelphia:

'I also will keep thee from ['out from' – i.e. never in it] the hour of temptation [Tribulation], which shall come upon all the world, to try them that dwell upon the earth. Behold, I come quickly'[154].

---

148 Rev. 6.10: 'And they cried with a loud voice, saying, How long, O Lord, holy and true, dost thou not judge and avenge our blood on them that dwell on the earth?'

149 Luke 23.34: 'Then said Jesus, Father, forgive them; for they know not what they do. And they parted his raiment, and cast lots.'

150 Eph. 2.15: 'Having abolished in his flesh the enmity, even the law of commandments contained in ordinances; for to make in himself of twain one new man, so making peace'.

151 Rev. 19.1-11: 'And after these things I heard a great voice of much people in heaven, saying, Alleluia; Salvation, and glory, and honour, and power, unto the Lord our God: For true and righteous are his judgments: for he hath judged the great whore, which did corrupt the earth with her fornication, and hath avenged the blood of his servants at her hand. And again they said, Alleluia. And her smoke rose up for ever and ever. And the four and twenty elders and the four beasts fell down and worshipped God that sat on the throne, saying, Amen; Alleluia. And a voice came out of the throne, saying, Praise our God, all ye his servants, and ye that fear him, both small and great. And I heard as it were the voice of a great multitude, and as the voice of many waters, and as the voice of mighty thunderings, saying, Alleluia: for the Lord God omnipotent

THE KINGDOM OF GOD IN THE TRIBULATION

 Paul explicitly taught that the day of the Lord... would come after the apostasy had taken place

To the Church at Thessalonica:

'*For God hath not appointed us to [Tribulation] wrath, but to obtain salvation by our Lord Jesus Christ*';[155]

'*Now we beseech you, brethren, by the coming of our Lord Jesus Christ, and by our gathering together unto him* [i.e. His return to the air], *that ye be not soon shaken in mind, or be troubled, neither by spirit, nor by word, nor by letter as from us, as that the day of the Lord is at hand*'[156].

Paul explicitly taught that the day of the Lord, which definitely encompasses the Tribulation period, would come after the apostasy had taken place[157]. The Thessalonians saints need not be worried and concerned by reports that this day had commenced. They were to look for the Lord from Heaven instead. They were safe from this Tribulation wrath.

A number of differences between the Rapture of the Church to the air and the manifestation of Christ to the earth are found in a chart in appendix 2.

---

reigneth. Let us be glad and rejoice, and give honour to him: for the marriage of the Lamb is come, and his wife hath made herself ready. And to her was granted that she should be arrayed in fine linen, clean and white: for the fine linen is the righteousness of saints. And he saith unto me, Write, Blessed are they which are called unto the marriage supper of the Lamb. And he saith unto me, These are the true sayings of God. And I fell at his feet to worship him. And he said unto me, See thou do it not: I am thy fellowservant, and of thy brethren that have the testimony of Jesus: worship God: for the testimony of Jesus is the spirit of prophecy. And I saw heaven opened, and behold a white horse; and he that sat upon him was called Faithful and True, and in righteousness he doth judge and make war.'

152 1 Thess 4.16-17 (C.f. Rev 4.1 in the context of chapters 2 and 3).

153 Rev. 16.11: 'And blasphemed the God of heaven because of their pains and their sores, and repented not of their deeds.'

154 Rev. 3.10-11   155 1 Thess. 5.9   156 2 Thess. 2.1-2

157 2 Thess. 2.3: 'Let no man deceive you by any means: for that day shall not come, except there come a falling away first, and that man of sin be revealed, the son of perdition'.

THE EIGHT KINGDOM PARABLES

What are the features of the Tribulation, prior to the Lord's return to judge the world?

A number of features will be true just prior to the coming of Christ to the earth. All these features have been seen at different times throughout history, but they will be redoubled in their intensity at this time. The Lord taught extensively about this period as recorded in Matthew 24, Mark 13 and Luke 21.

Seven features of the Tribulation:

1. **Anti-Semitism:** The Devil will single out Israel for attack, Jerusalem will be broken over 3.5 years and ultimately besieged (two thirds of the city of Jerusalem destroyed), but still spared[158].

2. **Religious Deception:** People will rise up making great claims to deceive[159].

3. **Military Propaganda:** Fake news about wars will be distributed to trouble people[160].

---

158 Rev 11.2: 'But the court which is without the temple leave out, and measure it not; for it is given unto the Gentiles: and the holy city shall they tread under foot forty and two months.';

Rev 12.13-14: 'And when the dragon saw that he was cast unto the earth, he persecuted the woman which brought forth the man child. And to the woman were given two wings of a great eagle, that she might fly into the wilderness, into her place, where she is nourished for a time, and times, and half a time, from the face of the serpent.'

Jerusalem broken down: Matt. 24. 1-2: 'And Jesus went out, and departed from the temple: and his disciples came to him for to shew him the buildings of the temple. And Jesus said unto them, See ye not all these things? verily I say unto you, There shall not be left here one stone upon another, that shall not be thrown down.'

Jerusalem besieged: Matt. 24.28: 'For wheresoever the carcase is, there will the eagles be gathered together';

Luke 21.20: And when ye shall see Jerusalem compassed with armies, then know that the desolation thereof is nigh.'

Jerusalem spared: Zech 13.8: 'And it shall come to pass, that in all the land, saith the LORD, two parts therein shall be cut off and die; but the third shall be left therein.'

159 Luke 21.8: 'And he said, Take heed that ye be not deceived: for many shall come in my name, saying, I am Christ; and the time draweth near: go ye not therefore after them.' (cf. Matt. 24.4-5);

THE KINGDOM OF GOD IN THE TRIBULATION

4. **Political instability:** Real wars between countries and power blocks will emerge[161].

5. **Geological and Economic catastrophe:** Natural disasters, pandemics and famines will multiply[162].

6. **Dissolution of family life/ Rampant individualism**[163]

7. **Persecution of Believers**[164]

We see all these features in embryo today, but they will be fully formed in the Tribulation period. What happens to the Kingdom in mystery at this point just prior to the second advent of Christ?

Will God's Kingdom grow in the Tribulation despite all this opposition?

Yes, perhaps the largest 'revival' the world has ever known will take place at this time. 144,000 Jews will be raised up by God and it would appear that they will begin to preach the gospel of the Kingdom[165]. These men will not marry but devote themselves to the work of God and will be

Matt. 24.11: 'And many false prophets shall rise, and shall deceive many.'
160 Luke 21.9: 'But when ye shall hear of wars and commotions, be not terrified: for these things must first come to pass; but the end is not by and by.' Cf. Matt. 24.6
161 Luke 21.10: 'Then said he unto them, Nation shall rise against nation, and kingdom against kingdom:' cf. Matt. 24.7.
162 Luke 21.11: 'And great earthquakes shall be in divers places, and famines, and pestilences; and fearful sights and great signs shall there be from heaven.'
163 Luke 21.16: 'And ye shall be betrayed both by parents, and brethren, and kinsfolks, and friends; and some of you shall they cause to be put to death.'
164 Luke 21.12: 'But before all these, they shall lay their hands on you, and persecute you, delivering you up to the synagogues, and into prisons, being brought before kings and rulers for my name's sake';
Luke 21.17: 'And ye shall be hated of all men for my name's sake.'
165 Rev. 7.4-8: 'And I heard the number of them which were sealed: and there were sealed an hundred and forty and four thousand of all the tribes of the children of Israel. Of the tribe of Juda were sealed twelve thousand. Of the tribe of Reuben were sealed twelve thousand. Of the tribe of Gad were sealed twelve thousand. Of the tribe of Aser were sealed twelve thousand. Of the tribe of Nepthalim were sealed twelve thousand. Of the tribe of Manasses were sealed twelve thousand. Of the tribe of Simeon were sealed twelve thousand. Of the tribe of Levi were sealed twelve thousand. Of the

THE EIGHT KINGDOM PARABLES

specially preserved[166]. A colossal amount of people will be saved; who will turn to the Lord Jesus for salvation and will not accept the mark of the beast. This is described in full detail in the book of Revelation[167]. They will all enter into the Millennial Kingdom. So, despite billions dying on earth through judgment there will be a vibrant, remnant, 'earthly' testimony being prepared to meet their Lord when He comes in manifestation with His Church from heaven.

tribe of Issachar were sealed twelve thousand. Of the tribe of Zabulon were sealed twelve thousand. Of the tribe of Joseph were sealed twelve thousand. Of the tribe of Benjamin were sealed twelve thousand.'

166 Rev. 14.1-4: 'And I looked, and, lo, a Lamb stood on the mount Sion, and with him an hundred forty and four thousand, having his Father's name written in their foreheads. And I heard a voice from heaven, as the voice of many waters, and as the voice of a great thunder: and I heard the voice of harpers harping with their harps: And they sung as it were a new song before the throne, and before the four beasts, and the elders: and no man could learn that song but the hundred and forty and four thousand, which were redeemed from the earth. These are they which were not defiled with women; for they are virgins. These are they which follow the Lamb whithersoever he goeth. These were redeemed from among men, being the firstfruits unto God and to the Lamb.'

167 Rev. 7.9-17: 'After this I beheld, and, lo, a great multitude, which no man could number, of all nations, and kindreds, and people, and tongues, stood before the throne, and before the Lamb, clothed with white robes, and palms in their hands; And cried with a loud voice, saying, Salvation to our God which sitteth upon the throne, and unto the Lamb. And all the angels stood round about the throne, and about the elders and the four beasts, and fell before the throne on their faces, and worshipped God, Saying, Amen: Blessing, and glory, and wisdom, and thanksgiving, and honour, and power, and might, be unto our God for ever and ever. Amen. And one of the elders answered, saying unto me, What are these which are arrayed in white robes? and whence came they? And I said unto him, Sir, thou knowest. And he said to me, These are they which came out of great Tribulation, and have washed their robes, and made them white in the blood of the Lamb. Therefore are they before the throne of God, and serve him day and night in his temple: and he that sitteth on the throne shall dwell among them. They shall hunger no more, neither thirst any more; neither shall the sun light on them, nor any heat. For the Lamb which is in the midst of the throne shall feed them, and shall lead them unto living fountains of waters: and God shall wipe away all tears from their eyes.'

THE KINGDOM OF GOD IN THE TRIBULATION

My Notes

What are the major differences between the return of the Lord Jesus to the air and the return to the earth?

Chapter 6

THE KINGDOM PARABLES – WHY PARABLES?

Matthew 13 records the eight Kingdom Parables. Several initial questions need to be answered before we look at each parable individually.

Why did the Lord tell eight parables?

Why did the Lord tell eight parables? Is there a connection between the various parables? The Lord uses the illustration of soil, seed, wheat and flour in the first four of the Kingdom Parables. Each parable stresses a specific aspect of the Kingdom, but collectively the first four Kingdom parables (the Sower, Wheat and Tares, Mustard Seed and Leaven in Meal) describe the **growth** of the Kingdom now, despite the evil and opposition. It is good to know that God's Kingdom will grow no matter what happens. Sometimes we do not believe this, and we lack faith. These parables encourage us and affirm our faith in God's Word.

The last four Kingdom Parables (the Hidden Treasure, the Pearl of great price, the Drag-net full of fish and the Householder's Treasure) describe the **value** of His Kingdom, despite all the counterfeit elements. They describe four things of great value to convey this thought. The Kingdom of Christ will be perfect.

Eight, of course, speaks of new beginnings. And that is certainly true as the *"mystery of the Kingdom"* reveals something new – the Church and the Kingdom in the Tribulation period.

THE EIGHT KINGDOM PARABLES

Why did the Lord speak these truths in parables?

The Saviour was asked: *'Why art Thou speaking unto them in parables?'*[168], and He gives His answer in Matthew 13 verses 10 to 17 and verses 34 to 35. This is an unusual section of Scripture and only explains why He spoke these Kingdom truths in Matthew 13 in parable form and not why he spoke parables at other times. Luke, for example, tells us why the Lord told parables. In the parable of the Pharisee and the publican it says, *'And he spake this parable unto certain which trusted in themselves that they were righteous, and despised others'*[169]: the story of the proud Pharisee praying with himself in the temple, contrasted with the tax collector, bowed down on his face, beating his chest and crying *'God be merciful to me'*, is extremely striking. The contrast between hypocrisy and authenticity is made to live in this parable. He also explained why he told a parable about prayer: *'And he spake a parable unto them to this end, that men ought always to pray, and not to faint'*[170]. The truth of persisting in prayer is vibrantly brought to life through this parable.

Sometimes a parable gives truth colour, form and lasting impact. Who will forget the story of the 'Good Samaritan' going out of his way to look after the man at the roadside?[171] Who cannot recall the moving scene of the prodigal son leaving the piggery to return to his father shouting, *'I have sinned'*[172]. We picture the father's love as he smothers his son with kisses, gives him a new robe, puts shoes on his feet, and kills the fatted calf. We now have a lasting picture of the love of the Father in heaven and His desire to bless us, despite our sin. Luke tells us why He told the parable of the rich fool – it was to show the evil of covetousness: *'And he said unto them, Take heed, and beware of covetousness: for a man's life consisteth not in the abundance of the things which he possesseth. And he spake a parable unto them, saying, The ground of a certain rich man brought forth plentifully'*[173]. Surely the story of God saying to the rich man, *'Thou fool, this night thy soul shall be required of thee'* teaches every person the solemn truth of the danger of putting material things before the salvation of our souls?

---

168 Matthew 13.10 **169** Luke 18.9 **170** Luke 18.1 -8 **171** Luke 10.29-37 **172** Luke 15.11-32
173 Luke 12.15-21

THE KINGDOM PARABLES – WHY PARABLES?

Therefore, the Lord told the Kingdom Parables, so that those who wanted to know the truth about the Kingdom would never forget it, and the stories would live long in their minds. Matthew said, '*All these things spake Jesus unto the multitude in parables; and without a parable spake he not unto them: That it might be fulfilled which was spoken by the prophet, saying, I will open my mouth in parables; I will utter things which have been kept secret from the foundation of the world*'[174]. The Kingdom Parables elucidate truth about the Kingdom that has been heretofore unknown ('secret'), and do it in a way that those who enquire will never ever forget it.

But a further reason is added in the Lord's answer in Matthew 13 as to why He spoke these truths about the Kingdom in parable format. On a first reading it appears disconcerting: '*Therefore speak I to them in parables: because they seeing see not; and hearing they hear not, neither do they understand*'[175]. It appears that He spoke in parables because they were refusing to listen. He then says that this unwillingness to listen to His word had been prophesied by Isaiah: '*And in them is fulfilled the prophecy of Esaias, which saith, By hearing ye shall hear, and shall not understand; and seeing ye shall see, and shall not perceive*'[176]. This is not just a lazy audience that is failing to listen carefully, but there is a deliberate turning away from the truth given by the Saviour: '*For this people's heart is waxed gross, and their ears are dull of hearing, and their eyes they have closed; lest at any time they should see with their eyes, and hear with their ears, and should understand with their heart, and should be converted, and I should heal them*'[177]. He wants to heal them, but they will not have it. Matthew 13 is therefore a pivotal chapter in Matthew's Gospel, when the Saviour says to the nation of Israel: 'Enough!' In Matthew chapters 1-12 the Lord had taught the Word of God plainly (Chapters 5-7, 10-12). His works had clearly demonstrated His claims in ten miracles (chapters 8-9). But Israel failed to believe and were condemned by the Lord Jesus in drastic terms in chapter 12, and warned that barbarians from Nineveh would judge them, and Gentiles from Africa would judge them for failing to see

---

174 Matt. 13.34-35 **175** Matt. 13.13
176 Matt. 13.14 **177** Matt. 13.15

THE EIGHT KINGDOM PARABLES

who the Christ really was[178]. So then, the remaining chapters of Matthew are spoken particularly to those who do believe or those who did not yet understand but wanted to enquire further. He said: *'But blessed are your eyes, for they see: and your ears, for they hear. For verily I say unto you, That many prophets and righteous men have desired to see those things which ye see, and have not seen them; and to hear those things which ye hear, and have not heard them'*[179]. Parables allow the believer to learn so much more than the world can ever understand. In some way, the 'parable form' of speaking was a judgment on those in the nation who were deliberately refusing to believe. The judicial judgment was that He could no longer speak in plain terms to them and would not do so anymore. Sometimes even when He spoke in parables, they understood[180] - but this form of speech allowed His disciples to understand and through enquiry learn more; it prevented riots hindering further teaching. The lesson here is that God sometimes takes our 'No' to be final.

How do we interpret a parable?

Four of the Kingdom Parables are interpreted by the Lord. These therefore provide a template for interpreting all parables. Several principles emerge:

(a) Get the big picture

The Lord never interpreted every detail of a parable; neither should we. In the Kingdom Parable of Hidden Treasure, we do not know, for example, if the man who owned the field knew if there was any treasure there. We know nothing about him. All we know is that there is a field in which some treasure was discovered. That is the big picture.

(b) Be careful not to apply the meaning of one parable uncritically to another

The 'seed' in the parable of the Sower is the 'Word of God', but the 'seed'

---

178 Matt. 12.41-42: 'The men of Nineveh shall rise in judgment with this generation, and shall condemn it: because they repented at the preaching of Jonas; and, behold, a greater than Jonas is here. The queen of the south shall rise up in the judgment with this generation, and shall condemn it: for she came from the uttermost parts of the

in the parable of the Wheat and Tares are the 'sons of the Kingdom'. We do not uncritically apply the meaning from one parable to another.

(c) Let the Scripture be its own interpreter

The Lord explained what things meant – for example, the Sower in the parable of the Wheat and Tares is the Son of Man. We must go with what the Scripture says and not make it up as we go along. If we cannot find Scripture to prove it then we must say we do not know, and it cannot be important to the main lesson. The Sower in the parable of the Sower is not interpreted. It therefore cannot be the focus of the parable – the focus there is on the types of soil, not the sower or the seed.

(d) When parables are packaged together then we should look out for the big themes

In Luke 15, three parables are told together – a lost sheep, a lost coin and a lost son. It is hard to miss the big theme about 'loss'. The four parables told in the house – treasure in the earth, a pearl of great price, a net full of fish, artefacts and things of value in a great house are all pictures of the value of God's Kingdom.

My Notes

---

earth to hear the wisdom of Solomon; and, behold, a greater than Solomon is here.'
179 Matt. 13.16-17
180 Matt. 21.45: 'And when the chief priests and Pharisees had heard his parables, they perceived that he spake of them.'

THE EIGHT KINGDOM PARABLES

The Kingdom Parables Overview
(Matthew 13)

NO	Name	Prominent Thought of the Kingdom
1	**Sower**	Salvation will take place and the seed of God's Word will germinate and true fruit will be evidenced in the life of all who receive it, despite the enemies of God attacking the sowing of the seed.
2	**Wheat and Tares**	The tares speak of superficiality in God's Kingdom – they are produced through enemy activity, using stealth. This counterfeit Christianity is all exposed by the Lord Jesus and eradicated at the end of the world. The security of the true believer is preserved.
3	**Mustard Seed**	God blesses a small grain of faith and His Kingdom will substantially grow despite such small beginnings.
4	**Leaven hid in Meal**	Serious doctrinal error is deliberately introduced into the outward manifestation of the Kingdom on earth and it permeates rapidly amidst the purity of the truth of the Kingdom.
5	**Treasure in Field**	The treasures of the Kingdom are unseen and then wonderfully discovered through the revelation of faith. The truth of the Kingdom is valued highly, cost God dearly, and remains concealed until the day of revelation.

6	**Pearl of Great Price**	The value of the Kingdom is sought diligently until the true priceless value of the Kingdom is discovered. Once discovered, everything else is sold to pay for it. It is all that really matters.
7	**Drag Net full of Fish**	The scale and variety of people in the professing Kingdom of God is in view. The scope, value, quality and purging of the Kingdom to maintain this purity is emphasised. At the end of the age the Kingdom will contain nothing that offends but be full of diverse types of people who have been saved by the Lord Jesus.
8	**Householder's Treasure**	The Kingdom is like treasure which is scarce (old) as well as modern (new). Selective revelation of the Kingdom treasures can be used to encourage God's people and instruct them in the ways of the Lord.

My Notes

THE EIGHT KINGDOM PARABLES

? *Why did the Saviour speak in parables?*

Chapter 7

THE PARABLE OF THE SOWER

The Parable of the Sower (1)

Matt. 13.1 The same day went Jesus out of the house, and sat by the sea side.

Matt. 13.2 And great multitudes were gathered together unto him, so that he went into a ship, and sat; and the whole multitude stood on the shore.

Matt. 13.3 And he spake many things unto them in parables, saying, Behold, a sower went forth to sow;

Matt. 13.4 And when he sowed, some seeds fell by the way side, and the fowls came and devoured them up:

Matt. 13.5 Some fell upon stony places, where they had not much earth: and forthwith they sprung up, because they had no deepness of earth:

Matt. 13.6 And when the sun was up, they were scorched; and because they had no root, they withered away.

Matt. 13.7 And some fell among thorns; and the thorns sprung up, and choked them:

Matt. 13.8 But other fell into good ground, and brought forth fruit, some an hundredfold, some sixtyfold, some thirtyfold.

Matt. 13.9 Who hath ears to hear, let him hear.

THE EIGHT KINGDOM PARABLES

The Interpretation of the Parable of the Sower

> Matt. 13.18 Hear ye therefore the parable of the sower.
>
> Matt. 13.19 When any one heareth the word of the kingdom, and understandeth it not, then cometh the wicked one, and catcheth away that which was sown in his heart. This is he which received seed by the way side.
>
> Matt. 13.20 But he that received the seed into stony places, the same is he that heareth the word, and anon with joy receiveth it;
>
> Matt. 13.21 Yet hath he not root in himself, but dureth for a while: for when tribulation or persecution ariseth because of the word, by and by he is offended.
>
> Matt. 13.22 He also that received seed among the thorns is he that heareth the word; and the care of this world, and the deceitfulness of riches, choke the word, and he becometh unfruitful.
>
> Matt. 13.23 But he that received seed into the good ground is he that heareth the word, and understandeth it; which also beareth fruit, and bringeth forth, some an hundredfold, some sixty, some thirty.

1. Behold a Sower Went Forth to Sow

Easy Everyday Lessons

The Lord commences His Kingdom Parables in Matthew 13 with a sower sowing seed[181]. He uses an everyday agricultural illustration that would

181 Matt. 13.3-9; 18-23.

182 Mark 4.13: 'And he said unto them, Know ye not this parable? and how then will ye know all parables?'

183 Dan. 9.2-4: 'In the first year of his reign I Daniel understood by books the number of the years, whereof the word of the LORD came to Jeremiah the prophet, that he would accomplish seventy years in the desolations of Jerusalem. And I set my face unto the Lord God, to seek by prayer and supplications, with fasting, and sackcloth, and ashes: And I prayed unto the LORD my God, and made my confession, and said, O Lord, the great and dreadful God, keeping the covenant and mercy to them that love him, and to them that keep his commandments.'

THE PARABLE OF THE SOWER

 All the great servants of the Lord asked questions

have been understood by all His hearers. This is a good lesson for all preachers of the gospel: keep it relevant and simple for every hearer.

Enquiry Blessed

In the first parable the Lord describes a sower sowing good seed and encountering difficulty when he sowed. In the wayside path the birds ate the seed; in the shallow soil the stones and rocks did not allow the seed to take root, despite the initial flush of promise; in the thorny ground the seed was choked from light and could not germinate. However, the good seed germinated in good ground and brought forth a wonderful harvest. Some of the seed had a 100% yield, others gave a 60% and a 30% increase.

To the enquiring disciples, away from the crowd, He explained the parable and thus set the structure for interpreting all parables[182]. God teaches enquiring learners. All the great servants of the Lord asked questions. Daniel, when he began to pray[183], made enquiry to God about Jeremiah's prophecy of Judah being in Babylon for seventy years[184], and he received a remarkable answer. The answer is found in God's revelation of His purposes for Israel over a 490-year period, in what we now call Daniel's 'seventy weeks prophecy'[185]. Zechariah enquired about the meaning of the golden lampstand and was given the astonishing answer of the power of the Holy Spirit[186]. It reminds us all of the importance of asking the Father to explain Scripture to us by the Holy Spirit.

---

184 Jer. 25.11-12: 'And this whole land shall be a desolation, and an astonishment; and these nations shall serve the king of Babylon seventy years. And it shall come to pass, when seventy years are accomplished, that I will punish the king of Babylon, and that nation, saith the LORD, for their iniquity, and the land of the Chaldeans, and will make it perpetual desolations.'
185 Dan 9.20-27
186 Zech. 4.4-6: 'So I answered and spake to the angel that talked with me, saying, What are these, my lord? Then the angel that talked with me answered and said unto me, Knowest thou not what these be? And I said, No, my lord. Then he answered and spake unto me, saying, This is the word of the LORD unto Zerubbabel, saying, Not by might, nor by power, but by my spirit, saith the LORD of hosts.'

THE EIGHT KINGDOM PARABLES

Explanation

As indicated in the introduction, the Lord Jesus did not explain every detail of the parable – for example, the identity of the Sower is not explained. However, He did unfold the meaning of the main picture in the illustration. The seed was good, as it was the 'Word of the Kingdom'[187], or 'the Word of God'[188]. The main lesson is that God's Kingdom cannot grow without the sowing of the Word of God.

The seed sown is the sole basis of growth for the Kingdom. The seed is good and there is no substitute for it as far as growth in God's Kingdom is concerned – a lesson to us for guidance on evangelism and spiritual growth. How much of our activity is based on the distribution and declaration of God's Word? It was the Word of God that Timothy's mother and grandmother poured into his little heart as it *was able to make* him *wise unto salvation*[189]. What else can parents give their children today? It was the Word of God that the Saviour preached[190], that Phillip preached[191], that Peter preached[192], that Paul and Barnabas preached[193]. Paul's exhortation to Timothy was that, after he had gone to heaven, Timothy was to *preach the Word*[194]. If we really believe that the Kingdom can only grow through the Word of God then let us tell it to our children; commit it to memory and quote it; put it on billboards and in newspapers; give away as many free Bibles and gospel tracts as we can; publish it on the internet; place it beside the hospital bed; preach it from the pulpits. It is the Word that carries all the power. Let us keep preaching the Word!

---

187 Matthew 13.19 **188** Luke 8.11
189 2 Tim. 3.15: 'And that from a child thou hast known the holy scriptures, which are able to make thee wise unto salvation through faith which is in Christ Jesus.';
2 Tim. 1.5: 'When I call to remembrance the unfeigned faith that is in thee, which dwelt first in thy grandmother Lois, and thy mother Eunice; and I am persuaded that in thee also.'
190 Mark 2.2: 'And straightway many were gathered together, insomuch that there was no room to receive them, no, not so much as about the door: and he preached the word unto them.'
191 Acts 8.25: 'And they, when they had testified and preached the word of the Lord, returned to Jerusalem, and preached the gospel in many villages of the Samaritans.'
192 1 Peter 1.25: 'But the word of the Lord endureth for ever. And this is the word which by the gospel is preached unto you.'

THE PARABLE OF THE SOWER

We often come under pressure to change our tactics or methods in a modern world – but no other alternative or supplement will work.

Engagement with God's Word

The first three soil types are: the wayside path, the stony ground and the thorny ground, representing three different types of hearers of God's Word. The 'wayside', the perimeter of the field and external path, represents the **disinterested** hearer who stays as far away as possible. Luke says they trample the seed under their feet before the birds eat it – i.e. show little or no interest in God's Word. The stony ground represents the **disillusioned** hearer who shows initial interest in the Word of God but who has not really counted the cost of obeying God's Word. They have no real convictions about things, i.e. have not the root of the matter. Whenever any form of persecution for the truth comes their way they are stumbled and lose interest[195]. The thorny ground represents the **distracted hearer** – the cares of the world and the attraction of riches have choked any spiritual interest. We find the same category of hearers today.

Now this is a simple illustration and we should not push it beyond what was intended. We know that sowers of seed in general do not deliberately sow seed on the trodden down wayside path. However, in this story it is an amazing thing that seed lands in all these soil types. In Luke's account it says, *'some fell by the wayside and some fell upon a rock'*[196] etc and the

---

193 Acts 13.5: 'And when they were at Salamis, they preached the word of God in the synagogues of the Jews: and they had also John to their minister';
Acts 14.25: 'And when they had preached the word in Perga, they went down into Attalia';
Act 15.36: 'And some days after Paul said unto Barnabas, Let us go again and visit our brethren in every city where we have preached the word of the Lord, and see how they do.'
194 2 Tim. 4.2 **195** Matt. 13.20-21 **196** Luke 8.5-15
197 1 Tim. 2.4-6: 'Who will have all men to be saved, and to come unto the knowledge of the truth. For there is one God, and one mediator between God and men, the man Christ Jesus; Who gave himself a ransom for all, to be testified in due time.'

THE EIGHT KINGDOM PARABLES

interpretation is given as *'those by the wayside are they that hear'*. The writer has found in his experience that those who vociferously oppose the gospel are often those who later repent. May we keep sowing the seed to all people[197].

Thankfully, the fourth soil type, 'the good ground', represents the **determined hearer**. When they heard the Word of God, they *'received'* it. This teaches us that those who will be saved need to receive and accept God's Word as final. They also *'understand it'*, accepting that they are sinners in God's sight, and they need to repent. They will accept that the Lord Jesus died for their sin on Calvary's cross and rose again[198], and that He is able to forgive them all their sins[199]. They are resting entirely upon His Word. Their 'assurance' of salvation is not based on anything that they have done, but on what Christ has done and simply His Word of promise to them. They believe in the eternality of His Word that heaven and earth could pass away, but His Word will never pass away[200]. No-one aimlessly drifts into salvation, no-one is born naturally into it, all must receive the seed of God's Word and be 'born again'[201].

Enemies

There are three enemies. The Lord Jesus explained that the seed was being attacked from **above** by the birds, barricaded **below** by stones underneath the soil, and consumed **around** by thorns obscuring the light. He identified the enemy above as **the Wicked One**, i.e. the Devil[202]; the hidden stones preventing root growth as those who have *'no root in*

---

198 1 Cor. 15.1-4: 'Moreover, brethren, I declare unto you the gospel which I preached unto you, which also ye have received, and wherein ye stand; By which also ye are saved, if ye keep in memory what I preached unto you, unless ye have believed in vain. For I delivered unto you first of all that which I also received, how that Christ died for our sins according to the scriptures; And that he was buried, and that he rose again the third day according to the scriptures:'

199 Eph. 1.7: 'In whom we have redemption through his blood, the forgiveness of sins, according to the riches of his grace;'

200 Matt. 24.35: 'Heaven and earth shall pass away, but my words shall not pass away.'

201 John 1.11-13: 'He came unto his own, and his own received him not. But as many as received him, to them gave he power to become the sons of God, even to them that

THE PARABLE OF THE SOWER

themselves'[203], a powerful picture of **the flesh** of our old unconverted nature; and the surrounding thorns as the '*care of **this world**'*[204]. This threefold enemy has never altered its character and it continues to stumble unbelievers to prevent any germination of the gospel seed and to strive with believers to stifle growth in the Kingdom of Christ. John could warn: '*love not the world*'[205]: its values, habits, mind-set, sport, music and politics will stumble sinners and prevent any Christian making progress. John also warned that the whole world '*lies in the Wicked one*'[206]. He was clear that the Devil was set against the believer, but he also believed that '*he that is begotten of God keepeth himself, and that wicked one toucheth him not*'[207]. Peter warned that the devil was '*their adversary*'[208], and exhorted, '*whom resist steadfast in the faith*'. Peter also warned that there was another enemy, that is, self or the flesh. He exhorted Christians that they '*should no longer live the rest of*' their '*time in the flesh to the lusts of men*'[209]. The first parable illustrates the three enemies who oppose germination and growth in the Kingdom and who must be overcome. All these enemies have been overcome by the Lord Jesus Christ in His death and resurrection. The Devil's power was disannulled at the cross[210]. The world was also crucified at Calvary[211]. When I come to Christ for salvation, I understand that the flesh must be crucified too[212].

The good ground hearers are those who have accepted salvation and are part of the Kingdom. This parable unlike the others is not introduced by "the Kingdom of Heaven is likened unto ...". All the other Kingdom Parables are a similitude of the Kingdom, but this is preparatory, showing

---

believe on his name: Which were born, not of blood, nor of the will of the flesh, nor of the will of man, but of God.'
202 Matt. 13.19 **203** Matt. 13.21 **204** Matt. 13.22 **205** 1 John 2.15 **206** 1 John 5.19 Darby **207** 1 John 5.18 **208** 1 Peter 5.8 **209** 1 Peter 4.2
210 Heb. 2.14-15: 'Forasmuch then as the children are partakers of flesh and blood, he also himself likewise took part of the same; that through death he might destroy him that had the power of death, that is, the devil; And deliver them who through fear of death were all their lifetime subject to bondage.'
211 Gal. 6.14: 'But God forbid that I should glory, save in the cross of our Lord Jesus Christ, by whom the world is crucified unto me, and I unto the world.'
212 Gal. 5.24: 'And they that are Christ's have crucified the flesh with the affections and lusts.'

THE EIGHT KINGDOM PARABLES

us how people are made ready for the Kingdom, that is, as a result of seed being sown.

Encouragement

However, the overall lesson in this parable is that **God's Kingdom will grow** despite the opposition! There was growth in the good soil in the field – one hundred[213], sixty and thirty percent increases[214]. This is an incredible yield. Let us keep sowing God's Word: there is no limit to its power. We can bring forth fruit despite the three-fold enemy of the Devil, the Flesh and the World. God's Kingdom will advance. He will always bless the receptive hearer of the Word. The different yields may correspond to the spiritual increase in the various phases of the Kingdom as it develops (Church, Tribulations saints, future Kingdom with Israel as the head of the nations). The different yields could also illustrate the impact of the three-fold enemy on the true believer's growth and enjoyment of the Kingdom.

My Notes

---

213 Gen. 26.12: 'Then Isaac sowed in that land, and received in the same year an hundredfold: and the LORD blessed him.'
214 Matt. 13.23

THE PARABLE OF THE SOWER

SUMMARY

- Keep Bible illustrations simple.
- God invites us to ask questions about Scripture.
- God's Kingdom will grow only through the sowing of God's Word. Let us keep sowing the Word and never change our method.
- We have three real enemies – we need to know them and their tactics.
- The Sower sows the seed to every type of hearer. God is not parochial or limited in His blessing.
- God's Kingdom will grow despite the opposition

REFLECTIONS

- Are we sharing the Word of God daily?
- Do we have any prejudices about those with whom we share the Word?
- Do we doubt the power of His Word?

THE EIGHT KINGDOM PARABLES

> **Blessed are ye that sow beside all waters, that send forth thither the feet of the ox and the ass.**
>
> Isaiah 32.20

Chapter 8

THE PARABLE OF THE WHEAT AND TARES

The Parable of the Wheat and Tares (2)

Matt. 13.24 Another parable put he forth unto them, saying, The kingdom of heaven is likened unto a man which sowed good seed in his field:

Matt. 13.25 But while men slept, his enemy came and sowed tares among the wheat, and went his way.

Matt. 13.26 But when the blade was sprung up, and brought forth fruit, then appeared the tares also.

Matt. 13.27 So the servants of the householder came and said unto him, Sir, didst not thou sow good seed in thy field? from whence then hath it tares?

Matt. 13.28 He said unto them, An enemy hath done this. The servants said unto him, Wilt thou then that we go and gather them up?

Matt. 13.29 But he said, Nay; lest while ye gather up the tares, ye root up also the wheat with them.

Matt. 13.30 Let both grow together until the harvest: and in the time of harvest I will say to the reapers, Gather ye together first the tares, and bind them in bundles to burn them: but gather the wheat into my barn.

THE EIGHT KINGDOM PARABLES

The Interpretation of the Parable of the Wheat and Tares

Matt. 13.36 Then Jesus sent the multitude away, and went into the house: and his disciples came unto him, saying, Declare unto us the parable of the tares of the field.

Matt. 13.37 He answered and said unto them, He that soweth the good seed is the Son of man;

Matt. 13.38 The field is the world; the good seed are the children of the kingdom ; but the tares are the children of the wicked one;

Matt. 13.39 The enemy that sowed them is the devil; the harvest is the end of the world; and the reapers are the angels.

Matt. 13.40 As therefore the tares are gathered and burned in the fire; so shall it be in the end of this world.

Matt. 13, 41 The Son of man shall send forth his angels, and they shall gather out of his kingdom all things that offend, and them which do iniquity;

Matt. 13.42 And shall cast them into a furnace of fire: there shall be wailing and gnashing of teeth.

Matt. 13.43 Then shall the righteous shine forth as the sun in the kingdom of their Father. Who hath ears to hear, let him hear.

2. The Parable of the Wheat and Tares

Summary

The next parable that the Lord taught in His Kingdom Parables also takes up the theme of sowing. The Lord taught that a sower sowed good seed in his field but as men slept his enemy sowed a weed (called 'tares' here thought to be 'darnel') that looked like wheat in his field. It was only as the crop grew it became apparent that this weed was amongst the wheat throughout the whole field. After some panic by the servants, who immediately wanted to root it out, the sower and owner of the field explained that this was the work of his enemy and instructed them to not touch anything, lest they damage the good crop. They were instructed to wait until the harvest, at which point the reapers would gather out the tares and burn them and leave the crop of wheat to be harvested into the barn.

THE PARABLE OF THE WHEAT AND TARES

❝ *The Devil is trying to spoil the world and the Kingdom and people of God*

Seeking explanation

This second illustration from agriculture has many fertile spiritual applications for us. On this occasion, the Sower experienced direct opposition from the enemy. The Lord taught the parable to the people but only fully interpreted it in the house after enquiry. The simple principle is that God will honour the honest seeker of truth: to those that have shall more be given[215].

Significance of Sower, Seed, Servants

The Lord Jesus interpreted seven parts of the parable to His own disciples:

i.   The Lord Jesus was the Sower - the Son of Man[216].

ii. The field was the world – He owned it[217].

iii. The good seed were the children of the Kingdom – that is those who had received the Word of God[218].

iv. The tares (weeds) were the product of the Devil - people who opposed the Word[219].

v.   The enemy who had deliberately sowed the 'tares' in the field at night was the Devil[220]. The Devil is trying to spoil the world and the Kingdom and people of God.

vi. The harvest was the end of the world[221].

vii. The reapers are angels – the servants of Christ, the Sower[222].

Everything that offends would be removed from His Kingdom and, at the end of the age, then will the righteous (as represented in the field of mature wheat) shine forth as the sun in the Kingdom of their Father.

---

215 Luke 19.26: 'For I say unto you, That unto every one which hath shall be given; and from him that hath not, even that he hath shall be taken away from him.'
216 Matt. 13.37 217 Matt. 13.38 218 Matt. 13.38 219 Matt. 13.38 220 Matt. 13.39
221 Matt. 13.39 222 Matt. 13.39

Lesson of the Sower

First, we learn about the work of Christ in His own Kingdom. Christ is sowing in His own Kingdom. This is a wonderful truth. He is the Sower and He is not passive in relation to His Kingdom. As we have observed in the previous parable the Kingdom has a present reality today. Our blessed Lord is sowing in the world today and those who respond to His work of love and truth will become '*sons of the Kingdom*'. We sometimes can get disappointed at the weakness of things; it is good to remember that God is at work in His own Kingdom and this very day many people will have come to Christ for salvation. His power is undiminished. We need to look with confidence at the '*fields which are white and ready to harvest*'[223]. Let us be careful lest we deploy language of despondency. Let us not diminish our appreciation of Christ's power.

Lesson of the Seed

In this parable the seed is not the Word of God, as in the parable of the sower, but we, the people of God, are the seed. (There is a good lesson for interpreting parables here – remember we should not borrow one idea from one parable and apply it uncritically to another parable.) The thought is now the value of the people of God and not so much the value of the Word of God, as emphasised in the parable of the Sower. What a high value the Saviour places on us![224]

---

223 John 4.35: 'Say not ye, There are yet four months, and then cometh harvest? behold, I say unto you, Lift up your eyes, and look on the fields; for they are white already to harvest.'

224 1 Cor. 8.11: 'And through thy knowledge shall the weak brother perish, for whom Christ died?'

225 John 3.5-7: 'Jesus answered, Verily, verily, I say unto thee, Except a man be born of water and of the Spirit, he cannot enter into the kingdom of God. That which is born of the flesh is flesh; and that which is born of the Spirit is spirit. Marvel not that I said unto thee, Ye must be born again.'

226 1 Pet. 1.23: 'Being born again, not of corruptible seed, but of incorruptible, by the word of God, which liveth and abideth for ever.'

227 Gal. 3.26: 'For ye are all the children (sons) of God by faith in Christ Jesus.'

228 Gal. 3.14-16: 'That the blessing of Abraham might come on the Gentiles through

THE PARABLE OF THE WHEAT AND TARES

We become children, or really the word is 'sons', of the Kingdom, through new birth[225], by the 'engrafted seed' of God's Word[226]. The word 'sons' always carries the thought of dignity, maturity and honour and not so much lineage or birth, as the word 'child' conveys. We stand in all the dignity, maturity, and honour of a son through faith: we are the *'sons of God by faith in Christ Jesus'*[227]. We represent our Father and display His features. The seed is called 'good seed'. We are blessed in Christ. He is the singular *'seed'* through whom *'all nations of the earth be blessed'*[228]. We are Abraham's seed by faith[229], even we Gentiles[230]. We should take encouragement from the fact that the Lord Jesus will preserve His seed. We know we sometimes fail, but here it is the thought of my position as a son in the Kingdom and not so much my practice as a son. As sons, we should reflect our Father's image. Let us have dignity then in our Christian walk and never do anything to detract from the glory of our Father.

Lesson of the Spoiler and his Strategy

The work of the Devil is to spoil the work of Christ in the Kingdom. The sower and owner of the harvest said, *'An enemy hath done this'* and the Lord identified him as the Devil. He is still working, seeking to spoil that which is of God. We need to be on our guard:

'Be sober, be vigilant; because your adversary the devil, as a roaring lion, walketh about, seeking whom he may devour: Whom resist stedfast in

Jesus Christ; that we might receive the promise of the Spirit through faith. Brethren, I speak after the manner of men; Though it be but a man's covenant, yet if it be confirmed, no man disannulleth, or addeth thereto. Now to Abraham and his seed were the promises made. He saith not, And to seeds, as of many; but as of one, And to thy seed, which is Christ.';
Gen. 22.18: 'And in thy seed shall all the nations of the earth be blessed.'
229 Gal. 3.29: 'And if ye be Christ's, then are ye Abraham's seed, and heirs according to the promise.'
230 Gal. 3.28: 'There is neither Jew nor Greek, there is neither bond nor free, there is neither male nor female: for ye are all one in Christ Jesus';
Gal. 3.6-7: 'Even as Abraham believed God, and it was accounted to him for righteousness. Know ye therefore that they which are of faith, the same are the children of Abraham.'

THE EIGHT KINGDOM PARABLES

the faith, knowing that the same afflictions are accomplished in your brethren that are in the world'[231].

The work of the Devil is subtle - it was done *'while men slept'*[232]. Just when we are at our most vulnerable then the Devil strikes. His work is often silent and unseen and often at night. His emissaries choose the same time to attack. The evil judge Abimelech certainly had the same tactics[233]; the king of Syria chose the night to come out against God's people[234]; the prostitute attacks at the same time[235]. Many a young person finds that sin lurks in the dark hours of the night, which is why 'early to bed and early to rise' is a feature of the godly. The Devil finds it so easy to get in amongst God's people – is that because we too are often sleeping? We need to be aware of his tactics. Paul says, *'we are not of the night'* and warns us: *'let us not sleep, as do others'*[236]. We must watch out for those moments when we are alone and not spiritually alert. That is when Satan strikes. The child of God must take steps to protect themselves when and where they know they are vulnerable.

It is some time before the fruit of what was done on that evil night becomes evident. It is some weeks and months later that the statement is made – *'An enemy hath done this'*[237]. How often this has been repeated throughout the centuries, as God's people have wakened up to the fact

---

231 1 Pet. 5.8-9 **232** Matt. 13.25

233 Judges 9.34: 'And Abimelech rose up, and all the people that were with him, by night, and they laid wait against Shechem in four companies.'

234 2 Ki. 6.14: 'Therefore sent he thither horses, and chariots, and a great host: and they came by night, and compassed the city about.'

235 Prov. 7.8-10: 'Passing through the street near her corner; and he went the way to her house, In the twilight, in the evening, in the black and dark night: And, behold, there met him a woman with the attire of an harlot, and subtil of heart.'

236 1 Thess. 5.4-7: 'But ye, brethren, are not in darkness, that that day should overtake you as a thief. Ye are all the children of light, and the children of the day: we are not of the night, nor of darkness. Therefore let us not sleep, as do others; but let us watch and be sober. For they that sleep sleep in the night; and they that be drunken are drunken in the night.'

237 Matt. 13.28

THE PARABLE OF THE WHEAT AND TARES

that the Evil One has influenced the children in their families, and years later his work is shown to produce untold damage. How much we need to be on our guard. His purpose is to produce counterfeit Christians and spoil the harvest for Christ. We cannot be too careful with what we allow ourselves to do, have in our homes and think about.

Please notice the limits of the work of the Devil and its likeness to the work of God. In the end he did not spoil the wheat but just produced weeds that looked like wheat. Not even the Devil can rob us of our salvation[238], but he does produce false and counterfeit Christians. Many an assembly has been spoiled because some in fellowship were never truly converted. Care must be taken that we never pressurise people into salvation – it often produces false professions. Let us be aware of the Devil's tactics, but also take comfort in his limited power. Let us look out for the characteristic features of authenticity (the wheat). The darnel and the wheat are different as they mature. Wheat stands straight and tall in the field and its golden grain speaks well of the Righteous One who owns it – so does the fruit in the life of every true believer. It is worth pointing out here that the field is the world and that is where the false and true grow together side by side. In the assembly of God's people, we should never assume that it is inevitable that false professors will be part of the company. That is why great care is taken around 'reception'[239] as ideally, they are 'Churches of the saints'[240].

---

238 John 10.28-30: 'And I give unto them eternal life; and they shall never perish, neither shall any man pluck them out of my hand. My Father, which gave them me, is greater than all; and no man is able to pluck them out of my Father's hand. I and my Father are one';
Matt. 16.18: '… upon this rock I will build my church; and the gates of hell shall not prevail against it'.
239 Acts 9.26-28: 'And when Saul was come to Jerusalem, he assayed to join himself to the disciples: but they were all afraid of him, and believed not that he was a disciple. But Barnabas took him, and brought him to the apostles, and declared unto them how he had seen the Lord in the way, and that he had spoken to him, and how he had preached boldly at Damascus in the name of Jesus. And he was with them coming in and going out at Jerusalem.'
240 1 Cor. 14.33: 'For God is not the author of confusion, but of peace, as in all churches of the saints.'

THE EIGHT KINGDOM PARABLES

Lesson of the Saviour, His Servants and His Strategy

We also learn something of God's ultimate purpose for His Kingdom. This parable graphically shows us that God's purpose for His Kingdom will be outworked. *'None can stay his hand, or say unto him, What doest thou?'*[241]. There is a direct application of the Parable of the Tares to Israel. They too have been spoiled by the Evil One, but God will produce a healthy nation – there will be a field of corn. The 'then' of Matthew 13. 43 (*'Then shall the righteous shine forth as the sun'*) anticipates the third of the three-fold 'then' of Matthew 24. 30-31 (*'then shall appear the sign of the Son of man in heaven and then shall all the tribes of the earth mourn, and [then] they shall see the Son of man coming'*). The shining forth of the true wheat in the Kingdom will take place when the Lord comes back to reign on earth.

The weeds (apostate Israel) will be destroyed and the nation will produce fruit again for Christ and be the *'head, and not the tail'*[242], and His enemies will become *'his footstool'*[243]. *'He shall bear the glory ... upon his throne'*[244]. The prayer taught by the Lord Jesus, *'thy Kingdom come'*, will be answered. This parable is also teaching that the Kingdom of God will ultimately triumph over all evil. God's purpose for all the sons of the Kingdom will be outworked and all that offends will be removed. One day, all that is wrong in this world will be put right and a *'king shall reign in righteousness'*[245]. What a day that will be.

We ought not to worry, then, when we see the opposition and the counterfeit and the evident success of the Evil One around us. In the current phase of the Kingdom we must remember, too, that the Sower said to Peter as He gave him the *'keys of the kingdom'*, *'I will build my Church and the gates of Hell shall not prevail against it'*[246]. God's Kingdom will be established, no matter the opposition.

---

241 Dan. 4.35 242 Deut. 28.13 243 Heb. 10.13 244 Zech. 6.13 245 Isa. 32.1 246 Matt. 16.18

THE PARABLE OF THE WHEAT AND TARES

SUMMARY

- We learn by asking the Lord to teach us.
- The Lord Jesus is sowing in His own Kingdom. There will be a harvest.
- The seed is good, and we are sons of the Kingdom – what value and dignity He has ascribed to us. What an honour it is to serve Him.
- We have an enemy in the Devil, and he works in an underhand manner.
- The Devil cannot destroy us, but he can produce counterfeit Christians amongst us.
- The Saviour will ensure that all true believers will be preserved and all evil eradicated.
- God's Kingdom will be established.

REFLECTIONS

- Do we ask the Lord to help us understand the Bible better?
- Are we ever despondent at the lack of interest? Do we doubt the power of His Word?
- Do we act as a 'son'? What does sonship look like?
- How aware are we of the Devil's tactics? What does his 'nighttime' work mean for us in our life? What should we be on the watch for?
- God is still on the throne!

THE EIGHT KINGDOM PARABLES

> **"Declaring the end from the beginning, and from ancient times the things that are not yet done, saying, My counsel shall stand, and I will do all my pleasure:"**
>
> Isaiah 46.10

Chapter 9

THE PARABLE OF THE MUSTARD SEED

The Parable of the Mustard Seed (3)

Matt. 13.31 Another parable put he forth unto them, saying, The kingdom of heaven is like to a grain of mustard seed, which a man took, and sowed in his field:

Matt. 13.32 Which indeed is the least of all seeds: but when it is grown, it is the greatest among herbs, and becometh a tree, so that the birds of the air come and lodge in the branches thereof.

The Parable of the Mustard Seed – Re-described

Mark 4.30 And he said, Whereunto shall we liken the kingdom of God? or with what comparison shall we compare it?

Mark 4.31 It is like a grain of mustard seed, which, when it is sown in the earth, is less than all the seeds that be in the earth:

Mark 4.32 But when it is sown, it groweth up, and becometh greater than all herbs, and shooteth out great branches; so that the fowls ofthe air may lodge under the shadow of it.

THE EIGHT KINGDOM PARABLES

The Parable of the Mustard Seed – Retold in a synagogue

> Luke 13.18 Then said he, Unto what is the kingdom of God like? and whereunto shall I resemble it?
>
> Luke 13.19 It is like a grain of mustard seed, which a man took, and cast into his garden; and it grew, and waxed a great tree; and the fowls of the air lodged in the branches of it.

3. Parable of the Mustard Seed

Summary

The Lord continues the agricultural theme of "sowing seed" in His third *Kingdom Parable*. On this occasion, however, He concentrates on discussing the sowing of one mustard seed. Although the mustard seed is regarded as one of the smallest herbal seeds[247], it ultimately grows into a tree several metres high.

Interestingly, for the first time, the Lord gives no interpretation of the parable. Indeed, He only interpreted four of the eight parables of the Kingdom. The spiritually minded will, by the help of the Holy Spirit, learn the main lesson of the parable from the framework of interpretation already given. The framework from the first four parables in Matthew 13 (Sower, Tares, Mustard Seed, Leaven in Meal) is clear – they describe the **growth** of the Kingdom now, despite the evil and opposition. The last four parables (Hidden Treasure, Pearl, Drag-Net, the Householder's Treasure) describe the **value** of His Kingdom, despite counterfeit elements.

Principle of Growth

The words '*and it grew*' or '*and it groweth up*' are the distinguishing words of this parable. The little mustard seed grew to be a tree, despite

---

247 The word is not 'least' in Matt. 13.32, as in the KJV, but 'lesser' where the thought is a relative and not an absolute concept.

248 Rom. 11.26: 'And so all Israel shall be saved';

Zech. 13.8-9: 'And it shall come to pass, that in all the land, saith the LORD, two parts therein shall be cut off and die; but the third shall be left therein. And I will bring the

THE PARABLE OF THE MUSTARD SEED

predatory birds. Therefore, the principle of growth despite the opposition is further exemplified in the parable of the Mustard Seed. In the first parable, the parable of the Sower, the Lord Jesus explained that the seed did not grow due to interference from **above** (birds), **below** (stones) and **around** (thorns). He identified the enemy above as the Wicked One, **the Devil**, the stones, below, as the **flesh** ("no root in themselves") and the thorns, around, as **"this world"**. The growth in the good ground has three possible yields – 100, 60 or 30%.

The Lord then typifies the work of the three-fold enemy in the next three parables - Tares, Mustard Seed and Leaven in Meal. The three-fold enemy is seeking to prevent growth. What is also documented is the ultimate failure of the enemy to destroy the final growth of the kingdom. In the second parable, the parable of the Tares, the seed grows despite enemy opposition from **within** (tares within, around and between the wheat). In the parable of the Mustard Seed, the seed grows despite enemy opposition from **above** (birds). Finally, in the parable of the Leaven in the Meal, the flour is initially unaffected but eventually it is infiltrated by an enemy from **without** (a woman).

Some have seen various phases of the Kingdom of God in these parables. The parable of the Wheat and Tares speaks of the Kingdom in its phase as Israel; one day all Israel will be purged and all the true Jews will be saved[248], and brought into a Kingdom on earth where they will *shine in the Kingdom of their father*. The parable of the Mustard Seed is seen as a picture of the Church phase, growing from the little seed of a few uneducated fishermen in Jerusalem and spreading throughout the world, despite huge opposition. The Lord said: *'I will build my church; and the gates of hell shall not prevail against it'*[249]. The parable of the Leaven in the Meal is sometimes viewed as the Kingdom of Heaven in the period where the Tribulation saints are on earth prior to Christ coming to reign. During

third part through the fire, and will refine them as silver is refined, and will try them as gold is tried: they shall call on my name, and I will hear them: I will say, It is my people: and they shall say, The LORD is my God.'
249 Matt. 16.18

THE EIGHT KINGDOM PARABLES

this time, apostasy and false teaching is rife and spreading like leaven; people are feigning to belong to Christ and stumbling true believers. Our blessed Lord warns of this in the Olivet discourse[250]. Although there are interesting parallels, perhaps, we should not over-emphasise this line until we see how all eight parables unfold. The overriding lesson is one of growth in the Kingdom, despite the opposition, in all phases of the Kingdom.

Principle of Faith

The principle of faith is also contained in the parable of the Mustard Seed - the emphasis seems to be on the growth of something so small and seemingly insignificant. The mustard seed had proverbial significance because people at that time spoke of things as being as small as a grain of mustard seed – for example, our faith[251]. There are two examples of our Lord using this phrase *'faith as a grain of mustard seed'*: first, when the disciples needed faith to heal the demon possessed boy at the foot of the mount of transfiguration, and second, when He spoke of the faith they would need to forgive their brother. So, we need faith to forgive as well as to function for God in difficult circumstances. Both are equally difficult.

The mustard tree grows tall, sometimes reaching five metres in height (some translations omit "great" in the text in Luke), and it is dense enough to provide shelter for birds to nest in. Nevertheless, it comes from a tiny seed. This parable reminds us that God can do great things through even the tiny faith of His people, just as five small barley loaves from a little boy fed over 5000 people on another occasion[252]. **We must learn the lesson that we too need mustard seed faith**.

---

250 Matt. 24.23-24: 'Then if any man shall say unto you, Lo, here is Christ, or there; believe it not. For there shall arise false Christs, and false prophets, and shall shew great signs and wonders; insomuch that, if it were possible, they shall deceive the very elect.'

251 Matt. 17.20: 'And Jesus said unto them, Because of your unbelief: for verily I say unto you, If ye have faith as a grain of mustard seed, ye shall say unto this mountain, Remove hence to yonder place; and it shall remove; and nothing shall be impossible unto you';

Luke 17.6: 'And the Lord said, If ye had faith as a grain of mustard seed, ye might say

THE PARABLE OF THE MUSTARD SEED

> ❝ *His kingdom...will grow despite the opposition*

The Principle of Purpose

The Context

Finally, the principle of divine purpose is also brought out in the parable of the Mustard Seed. The parable of the Mustard Seed is found nestling in the context of Luke 13, where a woman who has been bent for 18 years is healed, despite Pharisee opposition. Luke 13 is a chapter where a fig tree is fertilised and watered, despite prior fruitlessness, and a chapter where the Christ of God moves freely today, tomorrow and the day after despite Herod's (the fox) opposition. The parable of the Mustard Seed in the context of Luke 13, therefore, is underlining God's purpose that His Kingdom (Mustard Tree) will grow despite the opposition[253].

The Birds

The birds in the parable of the sower appear to signify demonic activity by those opposed to the truth. We do not want to borrow from the interpretation He gave in the parable of the Sower about birds, but, in the absence of any further statement from the Lord (other than what the Lord said about the birds in Matthew 13 verse 19 and Luke 8 verse 12), it would seem in this parable to represent demonic opposition roosting in the branches of the tree. In Daniel's prophecy the tree represented Nebuchadnezzar's Kingdom[254], and the birds in the tree those that benefitted in some way from his Kingdom (v. 12). The branches with birds do seem to indicate evil spirits ruling in Church counsels, benefitting from the protective environment of the Church on earth, whilst promulgating error.

---

unto this sycamine tree, Be thou plucked up by the root, and be thou planted in the sea; and it should obey you.'

252 John 6.9-11: 'There is a lad here, which hath five barley loaves, and two small fishes: but what are they among so many? And Jesus said, Make the men sit down. Now there was much grass in the place. So the men sat down, in number about five thousand. And Jesus took the loaves; and when he had given thanks, he distributed to the disciples, and the disciples to them that were set down; and likewise of the fishes as much as they would.'

253 Luke 13.18-19 **254** Dan. 4.1-37

The Branches

As Christianity grew, so many unbelievers attached themselves externally to Christianity, forming branches of what has become the corrupt and demonic system of Christendom. We can now look back and see, sadly, how clearly this prophecy has been fulfilled today in so-called Christian organisations and institutions – some of whom have committed gross evil in the Name of Christ. This 'branch system' is likened to a great whore in Revelation 17 and will be destroyed during the Tribulation period[255], when the counterfeit Church will be burned and looted by the Man of Sin to finance his military campaign at Armageddon.

The Tree

However, we must not miss the important point that the actual tree (God's Kingdom) still grew in God's purpose, despite the birds. This should encourage us today as we seek to honour the Lord in maintaining the simplicity of assembly of God's people, the House of God[256]. No matter how small we are, God will honour those who seek to preserve the purity and the pattern of His Word. The systems with all their branches and popularity do not have any future, whereas the angel said of the Kingdom of God that 'it shall have no end'[257].

In Mark chapter 4 the parable of the Mustard Seed is taught immediately after the unique parable of the growth of a seed[258]. The sower watches the blade, then the ear and then the full corn in the ear. He does not know how the seed grows ('he knoweth not how'). It seems to illustrate again the divine growth of a seed. God's Kingdom can and will grow – not by

---

255 Rev. 17.3-5, 15-17: 'So he carried me away in the spirit into the wilderness: and I saw a woman sit upon a scarlet coloured beast, full of names of blasphemy, having seven heads and ten horns. And the woman was arrayed in purple and scarlet colour, and decked with gold and precious stones and pearls, having a golden cup in her hand full of abominations and filthiness of her fornication: And upon her forehead was a name written, MYSTERY, BABYLON THE GREAT, THE MOTHER OF HARLOTS AND ABOMINATIONS OF THE EARTH . . . And he saith unto me, The waters which thou sawest, where the whore sitteth, are peoples, and multitudes, and nations, and tongues. And the ten horns which thou sawest upon the beast, these shall hate the whore, and shall make her desolate and naked, and shall eat her flesh, and burn her with fire. For God hath put in their hearts to fulfil his will, and to agree, and give their

THE PARABLE OF THE MUSTARD SEED

human ingenuity, not by human arrangement but by simple faith in God's purpose and will. We need to keep looking up. Our God has a plan and His purpose will come to pass.

SUMMARY

- The Kingdom will grow despite the opposition in all phases of the Kingdom.
- We need mustard seed faith.
- Our God has a plan and His purpose will come to pass.
- The counterfeit Kingdom cannot prevent the growth of the true Kingdom and has no ultimate future.

REFLECTIONS

- How big is our faith?
- Have we seen spiritual growth in our life? In others? What does it look like?
- What is my ambition for growth?
- What aspects of the religious 'branch system' encroach on our lives today?

kingdom unto the beast, until the words of God shall be fulfilled.'
256 1 Tim. 3.15: 'But if I tarry long, that thou mayest know how thou oughtest to behave thyself in the house of God, which is the church of the living God, the pillar and ground of the truth.'
257 Luke 1.33: 'And he shall reign over the house of Jacob for ever; and of his kingdom there shall be no end.'
258 Mark 4.26-29: 'And he said, So is the kingdom of God, as if a man should cast seed into the ground; And should sleep, and rise night and day, and the seed should spring and grow up, he knoweth not how. For the earth bringeth forth fruit of herself; first the blade, then the ear, after that the full corn in the ear. But when the fruit is brought forth, immediately he putteth in the sickle, because the harvest is come.'

THE EIGHT KINGDOM PARABLES

> **But speaking the truth in love, may grow up into him in all things, which is the head, even Christ:**
>
> Ephesians 4:15

> **As newborn babes, desire the sincere milk of the word, that ye may grow thereby:**
>
> 1 Peter 2:2

> **But grow in grace, and in the knowledge of our Lord and Saviour Jesus Christ. To him be glory both now and for ever. Amen.**
>
> 2 Peter 3:18

Chapter 10

THE PARABLE OF THE LEAVEN IN THE MEAL

The Parable of the Leaven Hidden in Three Measures of Meal (4)

> Matt. 13.33 The kingdom of heaven is like unto leaven, which a woman took, and hid in three measures of meal, till the whole was leavened.
>
> Luke 13.20-21 And again he said, Whereunto shall I liken the kingdom of God? It is like leaven, which a woman took and hid in three measures of meal, till the whole was leavened.

4. Parable of Leaven in Three Measures of Meal

Summary

The fourth parable of the Kingdom is the first occasion when the Lord did not use the figure of "sowing". The theme of "meal", however, reminds us of the ultimate purpose of sowing, harvesting, and threshing the grain of the field. In keeping with the agricultural theme, the first four parables of the Kingdom are all unfolded outside the house.

In this parable the story is remarkably simple: a woman deliberately corrupted three measures of meal with leaven. The leaven (yeast) then spread through the meal. The parable is again not interpreted by the Lord

THE EIGHT KINGDOM PARABLES

Jesus and the framework already given and the context must determine its meaning.

Surface Lesson of the Kingdom

'Three measures of meal' to an Israelite audience would have reminded them of the first meal that Sarah, the Mother of Israel, gave to the heavenly visitors and where she received the promise of bearing the sole heir, Isaac[259]. It is the only other time that a meal of this nature is found in Scripture. It would be a fitting picture of God's Kingdom and His abundant provision. The meal would be fine flour. The Meal Offering is described for us in Leviticus chapter 2 and had to be added to every Burnt Offering. For example, every bullock required three tenths of a measure of fine flour[260]. It was the fine flour of a Meal Offering that Hannah brought as an offering when Samuel was dedicated to the Lord[261]. The pure white flour would speak of purity and the holy character of God Himself, and of the manhood of Christ – characteristics which are also true of His Kingdom .

Hidden Lesson of the Kingdom

As with all the previous parables, someone or something external and alien to God's Kingdom is introduced into the Kingdom. In the parable of the Sower it is birds (above), stones (below) and thorns (around), speaking of our three enemies: the flesh, the world and the Devil. In the parable of the Wheat and Tares it was an enemy who deliberately sowed tares amongst the wheat at night, that lay hidden from view for so long. In the parable of the Mustard Seed, after the tree has grown, we have birds settling and roosting in the branches, and now it is a woman who deliberately places leaven (yeast) into the meal.

---

259 Gen. 18.6: 'And Abraham hastened into the tent unto Sarah, and said, Make ready quickly three measures of fine meal, knead it, and make cakes upon the hearth.'
260 Num. 15.9: 'Then shall he bring with a bullock a meat offering of three tenth deals of flour mingled with half an hin of oil.'
261 1 Sam. 1.24 'And when she had weaned him, she took him up with her, with three bullocks, and one ephah of flour, and a bottle of wine, and brought him unto the house of the LORD in Shiloh: and the child was young.'
262 Matt. 13.39
263 Matt. 16.6: 'Then Jesus said unto them, Take heed and beware of the leaven of the Pharisees and of the Sadducees';

The Leaven

Many have thought that the leaven is a picture of a good thing here and see the natural image of baking bread – a rising loaf (due to the yeast, leaven) as a picture of God's Kingdom expanding. However, this does not seem to be in keeping with the framework the Lord gave for the interpretation of the parable. He only interpreted four of the eight parables and we must use the framework given to interpret the rest. Although we fully accept that we cannot borrow an interpretation from one parable uncritically (and we have already pointed out that the 'seed' in the parable of the Wheat and Tares and the parable of the Sower are interpreted differently by the Lord), there does seem to be a theme of opposition running through all four parables of the Kingdom . The enemy in the parable of the Wheat and Tares, who introduced something foreign into the field, is the "Devil" says the Lord[262]. The "birds" came and roosted on the Mustard Seed Tree and are identified as the "wicked one" in the parable of the Sower. There is nothing to suggest anything other than that the leaven entering the meal in this parable indicates something false and erroneous. The woman '*took*', which seems to suggest a deliberate, preconceived action. She '*hid*' yeast in the meal, which appears to convey that it is something covert, and deceitful. The framework suggests that something foreign and evil is being introduced into something divine. Furthermore, a field of wheat, a mustard tree and three measures of meal are fitting pictures of God's Kingdom whereas tares, ravens and leaven (yeast) have no scriptural support for illustrating a holy thing. Finally, leaven elsewhere in Matthew and in our New Testament carries with it the thought of something evil. Whilst these Scriptures are not conclusive, they most certainly suggest that the prevailing symbol for leaven in Scripture is something evil[263].

Matt. 16.12: 'Then understood they how that he bade them not beware of the leaven of bread, but of the doctrine of the Pharisees and of the Sadducees';

1 Cor. 5.6-8: 'Your glorying is not good. Know ye not that a little leaven leaveneth the whole lump? Purge out therefore the old leaven, that ye may be a new lump, as ye are unleavened. For even Christ our passover is sacrificed for us: Therefore let us keep the feast, not with old leaven, neither with the leaven of malice and wickedness; but with the unleavened bread of sincerity and truth';

Gal. 5.7-9: 'Ye did run well; who did hinder you that ye should not obey the truth? This persuasion cometh not of him that calleth you. A little leaven leaveneth the whole lump.'

THE EIGHT KINGDOM PARABLES

The leaven of the Pharisees is ritualism[264], the leaven of the Sadducees is rationalism, the leaven of Herod is unreality and pride[265]. False teaching had entered the Kingdom of Heaven. The picture then of baking bread, and the loaf rising due to yeast (leaven), speaks of the permeation of false teaching in the Kingdom.

The Woman

The picture of a woman deliberately introducing corruption into God's Kingdom is certainly not without scriptural support. The corrupting influence of a woman can be observed in all three phases of the Kingdom before restored Israel is given the chief place in a future global Kingdom: Israel, the Church, and the Tribulation period. Jezebel and Athaliah are two Old Testament woman who sought to usurp the throne of God and to destroy the Kingdom in Israel. Both Jezebel and Athaliah came to a sorry end[266]. There are also examples like another Jezebel corrupting the local assembly in Thyatira and permitting and encouraging carnal behaviour[267]. The Lord intervened directly in this assembly to destroy her. The enemy is still at work today, leavening the assemblies of God's people during the Church era. The woman called the Great Whore in Revelation 17 is a picture of the counterfeit Church, full of abominations, and, as previously discussed, in the middle of the Tribulation she will be forcibly destroyed. The woman in Zechariah chapter 5 deliberately brings Israel into the idolatry of Babylon through commercialism and she is called 'wickedness'[268]. What religion and politics could never accomplish, she

---

264 Luke 12.1: 'Beware ye of the leaven of the Pharisees, which is hypocrisy.'
265 Mark 8.15: 'Beware of the leaven of the Pharisees, and of the leaven of Herod.'
266 2 Ki. 9.7: 'And thou shalt smite the house of Ahab thy master, that I may avenge the blood of my servants the prophets, and the blood of all the servants of the LORD, at the hand of Jezebel';
2 Ki. 9.37: 'And the carcase of Jezebel shall be as dung upon the face of the field in the portion of Jezreel; so that they shall not say, This is Jezebel';
2 Ki. 11.20: 'And all the people of the land rejoiced, and the city was in quiet: and they slew Athaliah with the sword beside the king's house.'
267 Rev. 2.20-23: 'Notwithstanding I have a few things against thee, because thou sufferest that woman Jezebel, which calleth herself a prophetess, to teach and to seduce my servants to commit fornication, and to eat things sacrificed unto idols. And I gave her space to repent of her fornication; and she repented not. Behold, I will cast

THE PARABLE OF THE LEAVEN IN THE MEAL

will achieve through commerce, but the day will come when she will be removed to her home in Shinar, Babylon and will be destroyed when the Lord Jesus returns – Revelation 18. In Zechariah 5 the element that is being introduced is commercialism; in Revelation 17 the corrupt relationship between religion and politics is introduced by the great whore. Here in Matthew 13 what the woman introduces is undefined, but it may well be, in the context of Matthew 8-12, the carnality of the Sadducees or the conceited legalism of the Pharisees.

Perhaps, therefore, the main lesson of this short parable by the Lord Jesus is to reinforce some of the main lessons of previous parables. God's Kingdom is pure (like the meal); God's Kingdom will grow (like the field of wheat and the mustard tree); God's Kingdom will come under attack and enemies will seek to thwart growth and damage progress; but, as the Lord will explain later in the house, His Kingdom will endure for ever and His enemies will be overthrown.

The Result

The disciples will have understood that the Kingdom of Heaven grew despite the opposition, but must have wondered why leaven was permitted to permeate the meal? Why were birds allowed in every branch of the mustard tree? Why were tares found in all parts of the field of wheat? Therefore, the Lord Jesus will now explain the parable of the Wheat and Tares in the house. He will show that the tares will all be removed, and

---

her into a bed, and them that commit adultery with her into great tribulation, except they repent of their deeds. And I will kill her children with death; and all the churches shall know that I am he which searcheth the reins and hearts: and I will give unto every one of you according to your works.'

268 Zech. 5.7-11: 'And, behold, there was lifted up a talent of lead: and this is a woman that sitteth in the midst of the ephah. And he said, This is wickedness. And he cast it into the midst of the ephah; and he cast the weight of lead upon the mouth thereof. Then lifted I up mine eyes, and looked, and, behold, there came out two women, and the wind was in their wings; for they had wings like the wings of a stork: and they lifted up the ephah between the earth and the heaven. Then said I to the angel that talked with me, Whither do these bear the ephah? And he said unto me, To build it an house in the land of Shinar: and it shall be established, and set there upon her own base.'

THE EIGHT KINGDOM PARABLES

it will become a fruitful field in the end. The professing Kingdom will be cleansed of everything that offends. He then underscores this truth with four parables (Hidden Treasure, Pearl, Drag-net, the Householder's Treasure) describing the **purity and value** of His Kingdom, despite counterfeit elements. The false system of religion will be eradicated and the Kingdom in all its purity and perfection will endure forever.

Likewise, after the parable of the Mustard Seed and the parable of Leaven in Meal is told in Luke's account, immediately the Lord explains that the Kingdom will be purified and all that is evil will be removed. He ends that chapter by stating that Israel will one day repent and say to Him, '*Blessed is he that cometh in the name of the Lord*'[269].

Sometimes God allows us to see the impact of evil upon His people today in the visible Kingdom. It should make us vigilant, especially when we know the enemies' subtle strategies. Their strategies are like the woman with the leaven or the birds silently sitting in the tree, or the enemy sowing tares at night in the field – they try to quietly and subtly rob the assembly of God's people of its purity and power. Peter says: '*Be sober, be vigilant; because your adversary the devil, as a roaring lion, walketh about, seeking whom he may devour: Whom resist stedfast in the faith, knowing that the same afflictions are accomplished in your brethren that are in the world*'[270]. But we should never forget that we can grow despite the opposition, and ultimately all evil will be eradicated from God's Kingdom. We are on the victory side.

My Notes

---

269 Luke 13.35 **270** 1 Peter 5.8-9

THE PARABLE OF THE LEAVEN IN THE MEAL

SUMMARY

- The 'meal' speaks of the purity of Christ as a man and of God's Kingdom.
- The 'leaven' speaks of false doctrine seeking to corrupt the Kingdom of Heaven
- The 'woman' reminds us of an organised principle in religion and commerce that is determined to corrupt the Kingdom of Heaven subtly but surely.
- The context for all four parables reminds us that growth can take place despite opposition
- The explanation of the tares after this parable reminds us that the Kingdom is eternal and pure, and all evil will ultimately be removed.

THOUGHT

- What does fine flour really speak of concerning the person of Christ?
- What is the leaven in our experience?
- Who is the woman today? What is she trying to do?
- What do we know of her future?

> **Ye therefore, beloved, seeing ye know these things before, beware lest ye also, being led away with the error of the wicked, fall from your own stedfastness.**
>
> 2 Peter 3:17

Chapter 11

THE PARABLE OF THE TREASURE HIDDEN IN THE FIELD

The Parable of Hidden Treasure (5)

Matt. 13.44 **The kingdom of heaven is like unto treasure hid in a field; the which when a man hath found, he hideth, and for joy thereof goeth and selleth all that he hath and buyeth that field.**

5. Parable of Hidden Treasure in a Field

The Private Place

The Lord Jesus now moves into the house. He told this parable to the disciples in private, having dismissed the multitudes[271]. The greatest unfolding of things of eternal value are normally given by God to enquiring believers in the private place. The Lord taught us to pray in private[272], and now He is teaching us to learn from the Word of God in private. Whilst

---

271 Matt. 13.36: 'Then Jesus sent the multitude away, and went into the house: and his disciples came unto him, saying, Declare unto us the parable of the tares of the field.'
272 Matt. 6.5-6: 'And when thou prayest, thou shalt not be as the hypocrites are: for they love to pray standing in the synagogues and in the corners of the streets, that they may be seen of men. Verily I say unto you, They have their reward. But thou, when thou prayest, enter into thy closet, and when thou hast shut thy door, pray to thy Father which is in secret; and thy Father which seeth in secret shall reward thee openly.'

THE EIGHT KINGDOM PARABLES

much can be gained from public preaching, nothing is more important than private reading and reflection.

The Purpose

The parable of the Hidden Treasure is the first parable told exclusively to the disciples in the house. As we have already observed, the disciples would have understood from the first four parables that the Kingdom grew despite the opposition, but they must have wondered why leaven was allowed to permeate the meal, why birds were in every branch of the mustard seed and tares in every part of the field. They must have wondered about the value of the Kingdom. Therefore, it was at this point, when they had come into the house, that the Lord explained the parable of the Wheat and Tares – all the tares will be removed, and it will be a fruitful and valuable field in the end. He then unfolded four more parables to illustrate this truth: the Kingdom was a fruitful field (vv. 36-43); a hidden treasure (v. 44); a unique and expensive pearl (vv. 45-46); an enormous catch of fish (vv. 47-50); and a householder's treasure (vv. 51-53). The Kingdom of Heaven into which they have been brought is of immense value to God.

This explanation confirms the view, then, that the first four parables in Matthew 13 (Sower, Tares, Mustard Seed, Leaven in Meal) describe the **growth** of the Kingdom now, despite the evil and opposition. The last four parables (Hidden treasure, Pearl, Drag-net, the Householder's treasure) describe the **value** of His Kingdom, despite counterfeit elements.

The Picture

'The kingdom of heaven is like unto treasure hid in a field'

The disciples would have understood the concept of hidden treasure in

---

273 1 Cor. 2.7

274 1 Cor. 2.8-9: 'Which none of the princes of this world knew: for had they known it, they would not have crucified the Lord of glory. But as it is written, Eye hath not seen, nor ear heard, neither have entered into the heart of man, the things which God hath prepared for them that love him.'

275 1 Cor. 2.10-14: 'But God hath revealed them unto us by his Spirit: for the Spirit searcheth all things, yea, the deep things of God. For what man knoweth the things of a man, save the spirit of man which is in him? even so the things of God knoweth

THE PARABLE OF THE TREASURE HIDDEN IN THE FIELD

a field, especially at a time when there would not have been any banks as we would know them today, and they would be aware that rich people sometimes hid their treasures in fields. (The Lord gave an illustration they would understand – a good lesson for those of us who preach!) Here was a field with a fortune and it was a picture of His Kingdom. Incidentally, the point of the parable was not to enquire after details. They were not told, for example, who owned the field or if the owner of the field knew the value of the treasure. Now, as with all parables, a main point is being stressed: God's Kingdom has real value and it is unseen and hidden to the eye of the natural man. The idea that spiritual truths are often hidden to the natural man but are revealed to faith is a theme throughout Scripture. Paul says, *'we speak the wisdom of God in a mystery, even the hidden wisdom, which God ordained before the world unto our glory'*[273]. The learning of this world cannot reveal these hidden truths[274]. Paul continues by showing that it is the Holy Spirit who reveals these truths to us. Divine revelation requires divine agency. An unsaved person cannot understand the treasure of the Kingdom of God[275]. Moses said that the *'secret things belong unto the LORD our God'*[276]. What a privilege that this treasure, the innermost thoughts of God are revealed to us. To quote Paul speaking of Christ, *'In whom are hid all the treasures of wisdom and knowledge'.*[277]

The Pattern

'When a man hath found'

These four parables told in the house always feature 'a man'; a purchasing man (buying a field); a merchantman (selecting and purchasing a pearl); a fisherman (casting a net – although in this case the fisherman is not mentioned, just the casting of the net which is significant); and a householder (bringing forth treasure). We believe that in all these

---

no man, but the Spirit of God. Now we have received, not the spirit of the world, but the spirit which is of God; that we might know the things that are freely given to us of God. Which things also we speak, not in the words which man's wisdom teacheth, but which the Holy Ghost teacheth; comparing spiritual things with spiritual. But the natural man receiveth not the things of the Spirit of God: for they are foolishness unto him: neither can he know them, because they are spiritually discerned.'

276 Deut. 29.29

277 Col. 2. 3

THE EIGHT KINGDOM PARABLES

instances the principal picture is of Christ. This is consistent with the framework of interpretation in the parable of Wheat and Tares which He interpreted in the house. He said the Sowing man was Christ (v. 37) and the field was the world (v. 38). Is it not wonderful to think that a man was sent into the field of the world to find and purchase something of infinite worth?

The Pleasure

'He hideth, and for joy thereof goeth ... selleth all'

The joy is associated, not with the sacrifice he made, but with the pleasure of obtaining what he had set his heart on – the treasure. This surely makes us think of another Man, our blessed Saviour, who for joy sacrificed His life that He might produce something of eternal worth: *'Who for the joy that was set before him endured the cross, despising the shame, and is set down at the right hand of the throne of God'*[278].

The Purchase

'goeth and selleth all that he hath and buyeth that field'

Can there be any doubt now that the man in the parable is Christ? We are never asked to sell all that we have and purchase salvation: salvation is a free gift[279]. However, in this parable, the Purchaser sells all to purchase the field. He had just explained to them that *'the field is the world'*[280]. Our blessed Lord has purchased and owns the title deeds of earth[281], and has paid the ransom price for the souls of all men and women[282]. The world

---

278 Heb. 12.2
279 Rom. 6.23: 'For the wages of sin is death; but the gift of God is eternal life through Jesus Christ our Lord.'
280 Matt. 13.38
281 Rev. 10.2: 'And he had in his hand a little book open: and he set his right foot upon the sea, and his left foot on the earth.'
282 1 Tim. 2.6: 'Who gave himself a ransom for all, to be testified in due time.'
283 Phil. 2.7: 'But made himself of no reputation (lit. 'emptied Himself'), and took upon him the form of a servant, and was made in the likeness of men:'
284 2 Cor. 5.19: 'To wit, that God was in Christ, reconciling the world unto himself, not imputing their trespasses unto them; and hath committed unto us the word of reconciliation';
Col. 1.20-21: 'And, having made peace through the blood of his cross, by him to reconcile all things unto himself; by him, I say, whether they be things in earth, or

THE PARABLE OF THE TREASURE HIDDEN IN THE FIELD

belongs to Christ by creation and by purchase. He has not redeemed (i.e. delivered) the field, but he has purchased it, and at what a great price! He *'emptied himself'*[283], and He *'gave himself'*, in order to buy the field and claim the treasure for Himself[284]. There is no limitation to the death of Christ. The Kingdoms of this world will become the *'kingdoms of our Lord and of his Christ'*[285], only as a result of Calvary. Whilst Christ died for the world, He also died for the Church[286], and the local assembly[287], and he also died for the individual, says Paul[288].

The Position

In the introductory chapters, the progressive development of the 'Kingdom' was traced throughout Scripture, including the Kingdom in mystery in the current period. As we have progressed through the Kingdom Parables, we have begun to see different pictures of the various phases of the Kingdom. This is particularly the case in the next parable of the Pearl, where we will suggest that the pearl might speak of the Church and the treasure here in this parable might be a picture of Israel. However, the main lesson from this parable is that the treasure presents God's viewpoint of the character and worth of His Kingdom, of which all true believers of all ages form a part. We have also noticed before that the Kingdom has a present manifestation in the assembly of God's people today. Let us treasure the place where God's authority is acknowledged, and His rule is known, for which He shed His own blood[289]. This is all hidden from the view of the natural man.

---

things in heaven. And you, that were sometime alienated and enemies in your mind by wicked works, yet now hath he reconciled';

1 John 2.2: 'And he is the propitiation for our sins: and not for ours only, but also for the sins of the whole world.'

285 Rev. 11.15

286 Eph. 5.25: 'Husbands, love your wives, even as Christ also loved the church, and gave himself for it;'

287 Acts 20.28: ' Take heed therefore unto yourselves, and to all the flock, over the which the Holy Ghost hath made you overseers, to feed the church of God, which he hath purchased with his own blood.'

288 Gal. 2.20: 'I am crucified with Christ: nevertheless I live; yet not I, but Christ liveth in me: and the life which I now live in the flesh I live by the faith of the Son of God, who loved me, and gave himself for me.'

289 Acts 20.28

My Notes

THE PARABLE OF THE TREASURE HIDDEN IN THE FIELD

SUMMARY

- God teaches us through our private reading and reflection on His Word, just as He taught them in the private place.

- The Kingdom of Heaven into which they have been brought is of immense value to God, like a field with a fortune.

- Just as the treasure was hidden, so precious spiritual truths are always hidden to the natural mind but revealed by God to His people through faith.

- The field which represents the world was bought, so Christ has died for all humanity and paid a ransom for every soul.

- God is now revealing to us the value of the treasure – His people.

REFLECTIONS

- Do we quietly spend time pondering God's Word?
- What 'hidden truths' do we enjoy?
- Have we grasped the extent of the price paid by the Lord Jesus at Calvary?
- What value do we place upon the people of God?

THE EIGHT KINGDOM PARABLES

> **In whom are hid all the treasures of wisdom and knowledge.**
>
> Colossians 2:3

Chapter 12

THE PARABLE OF THE PEARL OF GREAT PRICE

The Parable of the Pearl of Great Price (6)

> Matt. 13.45-46 The kingdom of heaven is like unto a merchant man, seeking goodly pearls: Who, when he had found one pearl of great price, went and sold all that he had, and bought it.

6. The Parable of the Pearl of Great Price

Summary information

It should be clear now that the last four parables of the Kingdom that the Lord told in the house (Hidden Treasure, Pearl of Great Price, Drag-net, the Householder's Treasure) describe the **value** of His Kingdom , despite the counterfeit elements. The Lord Jesus explained that the Kingdom was a fruitful field, a hidden treasure, a unique and expensive pearl, an enormous catch of fish, and a householder's treasure. The disciples would have been left in no doubt that the Kingdom of Heaven was of immense value to God.

Subject: *'A merchantman'*

As explained in the previous chapter on the parable of the Hidden Treasure, the purchasing man (buying a field), the merchantman (selecting and purchasing a pearl), the fisherman (casting a net), and the householder (bringing forth treasure) all speak of Christ. We are not the merchantman in the parable: salvation cannot be bought – it is a free gift[290].

'Seeking'

The Lord Jesus is pictured as a merchantman seeking something of real value. Is this not illustrative of the heart and purpose of God? He is seeking something of real eternal value on earth for His glory. The use of the word 'seeking' confirms that His investigation is thorough and not superficial. The shallow nature of popular religion is not something that will stand the searching eye of Christ. False religion, apostate Judaism or counterfeit Christianity will never satisfy the high standards of His rigorous search and testing investigation. Let us go in for the things that are real and be part of something of infinite worth. It is interesting to consider the things the Lord seeks in the parables – for example, a lost sheep is sought out by the shepherd in Luke 15 and a woman searched for a lost coin by sweeping the house. These parables remind us of our tendency to wander and of our vulnerability and yet our intrinsic value to God. Furthermore, the owner of the vineyard in the parable in Luke 13 is seeking fruit from a fig tree and not finding any. It is given one more year to produce fruit or else it will be taken down. The Luke 15 parables speak of the Saviour seeking souls for salvation and perhaps restoration, the Luke 13 parable speaks of the Saviour seeking evidence of salvation. Many will see a picture of fruitless Israel in the fig tree.

Suffering: 'Goodly Pearls'

He was not seeking gems, but pearls. Pearls are not from the earth but produced by the irritation of sand or grit between an oyster and its shell in the midst of the ocean. The pearl is therefore produced through the suffering of something living. Whilst we would not want to overstretch

---

290 Rom. 6.23: 'For the wages of sin is death; but the gift of God is eternal life through Jesus Christ our Lord.'
291 Eph. 5.25-26: 'Husbands, love your wives, even as Christ also loved the church, and gave himself for it; That he might sanctify and cleanse it with the washing of water by the word,'

...His sufferings produce glory

the illustration, is there not another principle here of the heart and purpose of God? Things of eternal value are always produced through suffering[291]. It is an eternal axiom that His sufferings produce glory[292]. Our Saviour suffered for our sins on the cross and produced something of eternal glory.

Pearls are also produced covertly, unrecognised by the human eye. The pearl is formed in the sea, when the suffering oyster covers the irritant with layer upon layer of nacre (mother of pearl). Another principle is that things of eternal value do not originate from the earth, nor are recognised by the world. They are revealed to the eye of faith[293].

Special: 'Who, when he hath found one pearl of great price'

There is only one thing worth having for this merchantman: a pearl of great price. The treasure in the field and the pearl of great price are beautiful pictures of the value that God places on His Kingdom. The language used of the value of the pearl reminds us of the language that God uses of the Church: *'That he might present it to himself a glorious church, not having spot, or wrinkle, or any such thing; but that it should be holy and without blemish'*[294]. When seeking to establish more precisely the meaning of the pearl, beyond the truth of something of real value in the Kingdom, there is a danger that we force an interpretation, and perhaps it is best to leave it there. However, there appears to be also a theme in these parables illustrating the various phases of the Kingdom. We would not press this too far but see a sequential set of pictures describing the progressive development of the Kingdom.

---

292 1 Pet. 1.11: '... when it testified beforehand the sufferings of Christ, and the glory that should follow.'
293 1 Cor. 2.14-15: 'But the natural man receiveth not the things of the Spirit of God: for they are foolishness unto him: neither can he know them, because they are spiritually discerned. But he that is spiritual judgeth all things, yet he himself is judged of no man.'
294 Eph. 5. 27

THE EIGHT KINGDOM PARABLES

Sequential Set of Pictures

In the parable of the Hidden Treasure in the field, the treasure discovered in the field and then hidden again could be a picture of Israel revealed in former times and then hidden again but awaiting the days of revival. Certainly, Israel lived in Canaan for thousands of years and then were hidden between AD 70 and 1948 – the country did not exist! They are also awaiting to be resurrected metaphorically and physically, as described vividly by Ezekiel in his vision of the resurrection of the valley of dry bones[295]. Certainly, Israel has a future and she will be restored as a nation; she is the Lord's special treasure out of all the nations of the earth to be His "jewels" of the future[296]. They will then be the head of the nations of the world and all nations will go to Jerusalem to worship[297]. The parable of the treasure hid in the field is therefore a very fitting picture of Israel.

The pearl, in the parable of the Pearl of Great Price, could also be a picture of the Church. The sea is often linked with the nations and the pearl taken from the sea could be viewed like the Church, the product of the living

---

295 Ezek. 37.1-3, 12: 'The hand of the LORD was upon me, and carried me out in the spirit of the LORD, and set me down in the midst of the valley which was full of bones, And caused me to pass by them round about: and, behold, there were very many in the open valley; and, lo, they were very dry. And he said unto me, Son of man, can these bones live? And I answered, O Lord GOD, thou knowest ... Therefore prophesy and say unto them, Thus saith the Lord GOD; Behold, O my people, I will open your graves, and cause you to come up out of your graves, and bring you into the land of Israel.'

296 Mal. 3.17: 'And they shall be mine, saith the LORD of hosts, in that day when I make up my jewels; and I will spare them, as a man spareth his own son that serveth him.'
Isa. 61.9: 'And their seed shall be known among the Gentiles, and their offspring among the people: all that see them shall acknowledge them, that they are the seed which the LORD hath blessed.'

297 Isa. 66.19-20: 'And I will set a sign among them, and I will send those that escape of them unto the nations, to Tarshish, Pul, and Lud, that draw the bow, to Tubal, and Javan, to the isles afar off, that have not heard my fame, neither have seen my glory; and they shall declare my glory among the Gentiles. And they shall bring all your brethren for an offering unto the LORD out of all nations upon horses, and in chariots, and in litters, and upon mules, and upon swift beasts, to my holy mountain Jerusalem, saith the LORD, as the children of Israel bring an offering in a clean vessel into the house of the LORD.'

THE PARABLE OF THE PEARL OF GREAT PRICE

Christ linked with the Gentile nations. The hidden pearl could also be a picture of the true Church which grows largely unnoticed by the world[298]. The pearl produced through suffering might remind us that the Church is the product of the suffering of the living Christ, even unto death[299]. The one unique pearl, like the Church, is a living organism, wondrous in its unity – a beauty and value that cannot be enhanced by human hand. The Church will be presented to Christ as a chaste virgin, *without spot or wrinkle or any such thing*[300]. The Church, like the pearl, is the only one of its kind – it is called *'one new man'*[301]. Every true believer is part of this Church. In Matthew 16 the Lord Jesus first announced that the Church would be built, saying, *'I will build my church'*[302]. The Church was established by the Holy Spirit at Pentecost in Acts 2, as discussed by Paul in his first letter to the Corinthians[303]. The Church, all who are in Christ, will be raptured home to heaven when the Lord comes, as recorded in 1 Thessalonians 4[304]. What a privilege it is to be part of something so special! The pearl, therefore, is a lovely picture of the Church.

---

298 Eph. 1.22-23: 'And hath put all things under his feet, and gave him to be the head over all things to the church, Which is his body, the fulness of him that filleth all in all'; Eph. 3.9-10: 'And to make all men see what is the fellowship of the mystery, which from the beginning of the world hath been hid in God, who created all things by Jesus Christ: To the intent that now unto the principalities and powers in heavenly places might be known by the church the manifold wisdom of God,'

299 Eph. 5.25 300 Eph. 5.26-27

301 Eph. 2.15: 'Having abolished in his flesh the enmity, even the law of commandments contained in ordinances; for to make in himself of twain one new man, so making peace.'

302 Matt. 16.18

303 1 Cor. 12.12-13: 'For as the body is one, and hath many members, and all the members of that one body, being many, are one body: so also is Christ. For by one Spirit are we all baptized into one body, whether we be Jews or Gentiles, whether we be bond or free.'

304 1 Thess. 4.15-17: 'For this we say unto you by the word of the Lord, that we which are alive and remain unto the coming of the Lord shall not prevent them which are asleep. For the Lord himself shall descend from heaven with a shout, with the voice of the archangel, and with the trump of God: and the dead in Christ shall rise first: Then we which are alive and remain shall be caught up together with them in the clouds, to meet the Lord in the air: and so shall we ever be with the Lord.'

THE EIGHT KINGDOM PARABLES

> **❝ ...what is certain is that there are distinct groups of believers in the kingdom...**

After the Rapture of the Church there will be a period of Tribulation and suffering in the world, as recorded for us from Revelation chapter 6 through to Revelation chapter 19. Although, as we saw in chapter five, this is a dreadful period in human history, with billions of people dying, 144000 Jews will be raised up and their preaching will result in a great many people being saved prior to the Lord's return in judgment[305].

The 'good fish' in the next parable, the parable of the Drag Net, could be a picture of the Tribulation saints being removed from the sea of humanity at the '*end of the world (age)*'[306].

We would not be dogmatic on this progressive view of the Kingdom that has been outlined in this section. However, what is certain is that there are distinct groups of believers in the Kingdom – Israel, the Church, and the Tribulation saints, i.e. those saved during the Tribulation. And it

---

305 Rev. 7.9-17: 'After this I beheld, and, lo, a great multitude, which no man could number, of all nations, and kindreds, and people, and tongues, stood before the throne, and before the Lamb, clothed with white robes, and palms in their hands; And cried with a loud voice, saying, Salvation to our God which sitteth upon the throne, and unto the Lamb. And all the angels stood round about the throne, and about the elders and the four beasts, and fell before the throne on their faces, and worshipped God, Saying, Amen: Blessing, and glory, and wisdom, and thanksgiving, and honour, and power, and might, be unto our God for ever and ever. Amen. And one of the elders answered, saying unto me, What are these which are arrayed in white robes? and whence came they? And I said unto him, Sir, thou knowest. And he said to me, These are they which came out of great tribulation, and have washed their robes, and made them white in the blood of the Lamb. Therefore are they before the throne of God, and serve him day and night in his temple: and he that sitteth on the throne shall dwell among them. They shall hunger no more, neither thirst any more; neither shall the sun light on them, nor any heat. For the Lamb which is in the midst of the throne shall feed them, and shall lead them unto living fountains of waters: and God shall wipe away all tears from their eyes.'

THE PARABLE OF THE PEARL OF GREAT PRICE

is also the case, as discussed in the introduction, that the 'mystery' of these parables cannot mean the final earthly Kingdom on earth, as that had already been revealed in the Old Testament and was no mystery. These sequential pictures affirm that the Kingdom continues in the past, present, and future.

Security: 'Who, went and sold all that he had, and bought it'

At infinite cost to Himself, the Lord paid the price upon Calvary to secure the redemption value of all humanity. This means he has the legal right to own every single soul, as He died a ransom for all[307], and salvation is now available to all because God is 'not willing that any should perish, but that all should come to repentance'[308]. However, as we have seen, the Lord Jesus also purchased the Church as His eternal complement[309], and He bought each local Church as well[310]. He paid, in the words of the parable, 'all that he had', or in the words of Paul, 'gave himself'. We are, wonder of all wonders, the complement of Him that filleth all in all[311]. What a price He paid in 'his own blood'. We will be displayed as 'the exceeding riches of his grace'[312] in a future day. What a value His Kingdom has!

---

306 Matt. 13.39-41: 'The enemy that sowed them is the devil; the harvest is the end of the world; and the reapers are the angels. As therefore the tares are gathered and burned in the fire; so shall it be in the end of this world. The Son of man shall send forth his angels, and they shall gather out of his kingdom all things that offend, and them which do iniquity';

Matt. 13.49: 'So shall it be at the end of the world: the angels shall come forth, and sever the wicked from among the just.'

307 1 Tim. 2.6: 'Who gave himself a ransom for all, to be testified in due time.'

308 2 Pet. 3.9

309 Eph. 5.2, 25: 'And walk in love, as Christ also hath loved us, and hath given himself for us an offering and a sacrifice to God for a sweetsmelling savour ... Husbands, love your wives, even as Christ also loved the church, and gave himself for it.'

310 Acts 20.28: 'Take heed therefore unto yourselves, and to all the flock, over the which the Holy Ghost hath made you overseers, to feed the church of God, which he hath purchased with his own blood.'

311 Eph. 1.23 312 Eph. 2.7

THE EIGHT KINGDOM PARABLES

My Notes

THE PARABLE OF THE PEARL OF GREAT PRICE

SUMMARY

- The Lord Jesus is seeking value in His Kingdom.
- The Lord Jesus suffered on behalf of His Kingdom to produce something of real worth.
- The Church is very special to the Lord Jesus Christ.
- The parables of the Hidden Treasure, Pearl of Great Price and Dragnet full of fish are possible pictures of Israel, the Church and Tribulation saints. They are types of the treasures of the Kingdom.
- The purchasing of the Church cost the Lord Jesus everything.

REFLECTIONS

- What value do we place on the Church?
- Are we prepared to suffer for truth?
- How do we see the progressive revelation of the Kingdom in these parables?

> **And hath put all things under his feet, and gave him to be the head over all things to the church,**
>
> Ephesians 1:22

Chapter 13

THE PARABLE OF THE DRAG NET

The Parable of the Drag Net (7)

> Matt. 13.47 Again, the kingdom of heaven is like unto a net, that was cast into the sea, and gathered of every kind:
>
> Matt. 13.48 Which, when it was full, they drew to shore, and sat down, and gathered the good into vessels, but cast the bad away.
>
> Matt. 13.49 So shall it be at the end of the world: the angels shall come forth, and sever the wicked from among the just,
>
> Matt. 13.50 And shall cast them into the furnace of fire: there shall be wailing and gnashing of teeth.

7. Parable of the Drag Net

The seventh parable of the Kingdom, like all the parables that the Lord told in the House (Hidden Treasure, Pearl of Great Price, Drag Net, the Householder's Treasure), describes the value of His Kingdom, despite the counterfeit elements. The value of a huge shoal of fish, and indeed of every type of fish, from a massive drag net would not have been lost on the disciples living alongside Lake Galilee. They would be in no doubt about the value of the Kingdom of Heaven.

THE EIGHT KINGDOM PARABLES

'A net .... cast into the sea'

The Man who sowed seed was interpreted by the Lord Jesus as the Son of Man. The Man who purchased the field, and the Merchantman seeking goodly pearls have all been identified as the Lord Jesus Christ. It would be consistent with this interpretation to understand that the One responsible for permitting the net to be cast into the sea was also Christ. He came to rescue men and woman from the sea of humanity. He said: *'Follow me'* and I will make you *'fishers [literally, catchers] of men'*[313]. In fact, no man is mentioned here in this parable, unlike the others; the fact that the net was cast into the sea is all that is emphasised. The focus is on fishing for men and women and not so much the One who calls us. Is our focus on evangelism and seeking to gather with our gospel net of every kind and type of person? Are we soul winners?

Although this parable could illustrate the preacher of the gospel casting the net of divine truth out in every generation, perhaps, as we explained in the previous parable, the "sea" here is the sea of the Gentiles during the period of the Tribulation wrath after the Rapture of the Church by

---

313 Matt. 4.19

314 1 Thess. 4.13-18: 'But I would not have you to be ignorant, brethren, concerning them which are asleep, that ye sorrow not, even as others which have no hope. 14For if we believe that Jesus died and rose again, even so them also which sleep in Jesus will God bring with him. For this we say unto you by the word of the Lord, that we which are alive and remain unto the coming of the Lord shall not prevent them which are asleep. For the Lord himself shall descend from heaven with a shout, with the voice of the archangel, and with the trump of God: and the dead in Christ shall rise first: Then we which are alive and remain shall be caught up together with them in the clouds, to meet the Lord in the air: and so shall we ever be with the Lord. Wherefore comfort one another with these words.'

315 1 Thess. 5. 9: 'For God hath not appointed us to wrath, but to obtain salvation by our Lord Jesus Christ,'

316 Rev. 7.4-8: 'And I heard the number of them which were sealed: and there were sealed an hundred and forty and four thousand of all the tribes of the children of Israel. Of the tribe of Juda were sealed twelve thousand. Of the tribe of Reuben were sealed twelve thousand. Of the tribe of Gad were sealed twelve thousand. Of the tribe of Aser were sealed twelve thousand. Of the tribe of Nepthalim were sealed twelve thousand. Of the tribe of Manasses were sealed twelve thousand. Of the tribe of Simeon were sealed twelve thousand. Of the tribe of Levi were sealed twelve thousand. Of the tribe of Issachar were sealed twelve thousand. Of the tribe of Zabulon were sealed

THE PARABLE OF THE DRAG NET

the Lord Jesus. If the "treasure" is a possible type of Israel and the "pearl" a picture of the Church, then the "drag net" would be demonstrating the third phase of the Kingdom, in the Tribulation period, after the Lord Jesus' return to the air for the Church[314]. Paul taught that the Church would not go through the period of Tribulation wrath (see chapter five and Appendix 2)[315]. After the Rapture, the Tribulation commences and 144,000 men, who are "Jews" are anointed[316]. Although we cannot be dogmatic, it would appear that the 144,000 are preachers of the gospel of the Kingdom in the world. Whether or not they are preachers, it is certainly true that an extremely large number of souls are saved[317].

'Gathered of every kind'

This large drag net, which is often dragged between two boats, gathers of 'every kind' of fish and is ultimately *'full'*. God is not parochial and has no favourites[318] – His net was cast into the sea and gathered of *every kind*. The Lord said, '**Whosoever** *believeth in him should not perish but have everlasting life'*. No one can ever claim that there was no salvation for

---

twelve thousand. Of the tribe of Joseph were sealed twelve thousand. Of the tribe of Benjamin were sealed twelve thousand.'

317 Rev. 7.9-17: 'After this I beheld, and, lo, a great multitude, which no man could number, of all nations, and kindreds, and people, and tongues, stood before the throne, and before the Lamb, clothed with white robes, and palms in their hands; And cried with a loud voice, saying, Salvation to our God which sitteth upon the throne, and unto the Lamb. And all the angels stood round about the throne, and about the elders and the four beasts, and fell before the throne on their faces, and worshipped God, Saying, Amen: Blessing, and glory, and wisdom, and thanksgiving, and honour, and power, and might, be unto our God for ever and ever. Amen. And one of the elders answered, saying unto me, What are these which are arrayed in white robes? and whence came they? And I said unto him, Sir, thou knowest. And he said to me, These are they which came out of great tribulation, and have washed their robes, and made them white in the blood of the Lamb. Therefore are they before the throne of God, and serve him day and night in his temple: and he that sitteth on the throne shall dwell among them. They shall hunger no more, neither thirst any more; neither shall the sun light on them, nor any heat. For the Lamb which is in the midst of the throne shall feed them, and shall lead them unto living fountains of waters: and God shall wipe away all tears from their eyes.'

318 Acts 10.34: 'Then Peter opened his mouth, and said, Of a truth I perceive that God is no respecter of persons.'

THE EIGHT KINGDOM PARABLES

them. The death of Christ is *'for all'*. He *'died as a ransom for all'*[319]. No one is exempt – all can be saved. Paul believed the sea was full of fish, *'I am made all things to all men, that I might by all means save some'*[320]. Paul was carrying out his divinely given commission and preaching the gospel to all the world – the net was cast into the sea at large. Are we still doing this? Or have we given up and succumbed to unbelief?

'Which, when it was full'

There will, solemnly, be a day when the gospel net will be full and brought up for the very last time. God is longsuffering, but there is a reckoning day.

'they drew to shore, and sat down, and gathered the good into vessels'

The reapers are the angels in the parable of the Wheat and Tares and those drawing the fish to the shore are also angels as interpreted by the Lord in the next verse. Therefore the *'they'* in the verse above are *'angels'*. Angels cannot save but they rejoice in our salvation[321], and they can *'minister'* to those who are *'heirs of salvation'*[322]. Angels are observing[323] those who are *'gathered'* out in fellowship to the Lord Jesus alone, upholding the doctrine of Christ, and support them in their separation. Indeed, the assembly of God's people can teach angels[324] the *'wisdom of God'* and know divine protection. This protection in their separation

---

319 1 Tim. 2.6 **320** 1 Cor. 9.22
321 Luke 15.10: 'Likewise, I say unto you, there is joy in the presence of the angels of God over one sinner that repenteth.'
322 Heb. 1.14: 'Are they not all ministering spirits, sent forth to minister for them who shall be heirs of salvation?'
323 1 Cor. 11.10: 'For this cause ought the woman to have power on her head because of the angels';
1 Tim. 5.21: 'I charge thee before God, and the Lord Jesus Christ, and the elect angels, that thou observe these things without preferring one before another, doing nothing by partiality.'
324 Eph. 3.10: 'To the intent that now unto the principalities and powers in heavenly places might be known by [through] the Church the manifold wisdom of God.'
325 Romans 3.23, 12

THE PARABLE OF THE DRAG NET

is perhaps hinted at, when the good fish are *'gathered'* and the *'good'* separated *'into vessels'*.

'but cast the bad away'

The angels can also, as we have seen already in the parable of the Wheat and Tares, be instruments of judgment: *'cast the bad away'*. The *'good fish'* are the truly saved and not those masquerading as being saved. Everything that corrupts and is not truly saved (the bad fish) will be removed. *'All have sinned'* and *'there is none that doeth good'* is the testimony of Scripture[325]; so all are *bad* in that sense. The *'good'* here, therefore, are those who have accepted the Lord Jesus as Saviour: it is not the thought of intrinsic goodness. This is not saved people being cast away for personal failure. Never! Once we are saved, we are always saved: it is impossible to lose your salvation[326]. During the Tribulation period the Lord warned that there would be many counterfeit and apostate believers[327]; these could be the meaning of the bad fish.

'... the angels shall come forth, and sever the wicked from among the just. And shall cast them into the furnace of fire: there shall be wailing and gnashing of teeth.'

The linking of angels with judgment is also to be found at the judgment of the living nations[328]. This is a tribunal set up after the Lord comes, to remove everything that offends from his Kingdom on a righteous basis.

---

326 John 10.28-30: 'And I give unto them eternal life; and they shall never perish, neither shall any man pluck them out of my hand. My Father, which gave them me, is greater than all; and no man is able to pluck them out of my Father's hand. I and my Father are one.'

327 Matt. 24.10-11: 'And then shall many be offended, and shall betray one another, and shall hate one another. And many false prophets shall rise, and shall deceive many.'

328 Matt. 25.31-33: 'When the Son of man shall come in his glory, and all the holy angels with him, then shall he sit upon the throne of his glory: And before him shall be gathered all nations: and he shall separate them one from another, as a shepherd divideth his sheep from the goats. And he shall set the sheep on his right hand, but the goats on the left.'

THE EIGHT KINGDOM PARABLES

The angels assist the judicial process following Christ's second advent, just prior to the inauguration of the messianic Kingdom on earth[329].

'So shall it be at the end of the world'

The fullest explanation of this parable, like the parable of the Wheat and Tares, is at the 'end of the age'. It points to the end of the Tribulation period when the Lord Jesus returns to reign and those faithful to Christ will be separated from the counterfeit. The field of wheat will be complete with no tares; the treasure will be found in the field; the pearl of great price will be spotted amongst all the other pearls rendering all the other pearls of no worth, and the fish are now all good fish. Like the Kingdom, the field of wheat, the treasure, the pearl or the large shoal of fish will be perfect in the end. What eternal value there is in the Kingdom of Heaven.

My Notes

---

329 2 Thess. 1.7: 'And to you who are troubled rest with us, when the Lord Jesus shall be revealed from heaven with his mighty angels,'

THE PARABLE OF THE DRAG NET

SUMMARY

- The Lord Jesus is asking us to cast the net and fish for men and women.
- The Kingdom will be of every kind: we should not be parochial in our gospel preaching. We preach 'whosoever'.
- There will, solemnly, be a day when the net will be full and never cast again.
- At the end of the Tribulation period angels will remove the false and those masquerading as Christians but deliver the true to safety.
- The Kingdom of Heaven has real value pictured in the value of a heaving net of beautiful fish freshly drawn from the sea.

REFLECTIONS

- What value do we place on evangelism?
- Do we go after every type of person for Christ?
- Will people be saved in the Tribulation period? How?

> **And Jesus said unto them, Come ye after me, and I will make you to become fishers of men.**
>
> Mark 1:17

Chapter 14

THE PARABLE OF THE HOUSEHOLDER

The Parable of the Householder (8)

> Matt. 13.51 Jesus saith unto them, Have ye understood all these things? They say unto him, Yea, Lord.
>
> Matt. 13.52 Then said he unto them, Therefore every scribe which is instructed unto the kingdom of heaven is like unto a man that is an householder, which bringeth forth out of his treasure things new and old.
>
> Matt. 13.53 And it came to pass, that when Jesus had finished these parables, he departed thence.

8. Parable of the Householder

The eighth and final parable of the Kingdom, like all the other parables that the Lord told in the house (i.e. 'Hidden Treasure', 'the Pearl of Great Price', and the 'Drag Net'), describes the **value** of His Kingdom . On this occasion the imagery used of the Kingdom is "treasure" in a house (i.e. objects of value in a great house), which was previously hidden but is now revealed.

However, the main figure of the previous parables, which was Christ (as a Sower, Purchaser, Merchantman, Fisherman), now moves to the disciples

THE EIGHT KINGDOM PARABLES

as 'scribes instructed unto the kingdom of heaven'. The value is now the disciple's learning and appreciation of the wealth and the use made of the treasures of the Kingdom for the glory of God.

'Have you understood all these things?'

The disciples now had greater revelation, as He had unfolded seven Kingdom Parables to them and explained three of them. He asks the disciples, 'Have you understood all these things?' He did not ask if they had "heard all these things". His question was deeper: did they have a spiritual understanding of what He had been teaching? As disciples, we must learn to take these challenges from the Lord seriously. In response to this question of their comprehension of the parables, the disciples chorus, 'Yea, Lord'. They had previously asked Him to explain the parable of the sower[330], but they now seem confident that they had understood all seven parables! We should be honest in the presence of God if we do not understand. Had they understood that some of the parables' fullest explanation lay in Israel's testimony in the last days prior to the coming of the Messiah at the "end of the age" (also called the Tribulation period) and the ushering in of His physical Kingdom on earth? Had they understood the necessity of the sacrifice of Christ in His death that underpinned the meaning of the parables, for example, the purchasing of the field and the pearl of great price? Had they understood that all the parables ended at the 'end of the age'? These parables were not describing the physical Kingdom of God to which they looked forward from Old Testament Scriptures. Rather, the Kingdom parables were a mystery and had a meaning for the here and now, with much of their interpretation contemporaneous with this present age: did they realise that God was preparing them for the present phase of the Kingdom in the Church period?

---

330 Mark 4.10, 13: 'And when he was alone, they that were about him with the twelve asked of him the parable ... And he said unto them, Know ye not this parable? and how then will ye know all parables?'

331 Eph. 1.13: 'In whom ye also trusted, after that ye heard the word of truth, the gospel of your salvation: in whom also after that ye believed, ye were sealed with that holy Spirit of promise,'

THE PARABLE OF THE HOUSEHOLDER

Perhaps we, with the indwelling Holy Spirit[331] and the complete canon of Holy Scripture, can see truth that they could not then fully comprehend. We also feel sure that we too often say, *'Yea, Lord'* when God would have us to understand deeper lessons of His purpose and will. It is interesting, in Matthew, how often the Lord gently but authoritatively corrected this attitude, repeatedly saying, *'Do ye not understand?'*[332] There are parallels with Paul's *'Know ye not'* in his letter to the Corinthians who felt that they had a superior attitude in spiritual things.

'Every scribe which is instructed unto the Kingdom of Heaven'

Greater light brings greater responsibility. The scribes, instructed in His teaching about the Kingdom of Heaven, should be able to draw on the treasure store of spiritual truth, to teach others. They should, for example, be able to appreciate Old Testament prophecies concerning the future Millennial Kingdom and draw on the new teachings of Christ regarding the current aspect of the Kingdom in the Church.

'is like unto a man that is an householder, which bringeth forth out of his treasure things new and old'

It is 'new and old', not 'old and new'. The order is important. It is when we apply the New Testament light to the page of the Old Testament that the gems of Holy Scripture are uncovered. We are also learning in this last parable the value of God's Word which we must appreciate if we are to be scribes encouraging others of the greatness of the Kingdom. It is often said that people today know the price of everything and the value of nothing. Truth has to be bought; trophies have to be won; treasure has to be mined. The Householder knows the value of the items in his house and chooses carefully what he brings out to give or share with

---

332 Matt. 15.17: 'Do not ye yet understand, that whatsoever entereth in at the mouth goeth into the belly, and is cast out into the draught?;
Matt. 16.9: 'Do ye not yet understand, neither remember the five loaves of the five thousand, and how many baskets ye took up?' (see also v. 11);
Matt. 22.29: 'Jesus answered and said unto them, Ye do err, not knowing the scriptures, nor the power of God.'

others. As scribes we need to learn the value of His Word and use it for the advancement of the Kingdom. We must learn that old truth, like old artifacts, can have real value. In God's Word some of the oldest truth, for example, the Offerings or the Tabernacle, in the light of New Testament teaching, are of inestimable value, particularly for worship. The old truth in this context may well be the truth of the Kingdom on earth which was well rehearsed in Old Testament Scriptures. The new truth might be the Kingdom in mystery, as revealed in the New Testament in the period of Christ's absence from earth.

The challenge to us is, do we understand all these things? Are we capable of delving into the storehouse of Scripture to teach others? Do we accept the principle that the greater the revelation of God from His Word, the greater our obligation to do as the Lord instructed the disciples?

'when Jesus had finished these parables'

These eight precious Kingdom Parables from the Saviour are an unfolding of God's eternal purpose and of the principles that currently mark and will permanently feature in His Kingdom.

My Notes

THE PARABLE OF THE HOUSEHOLDER

SUMMARY

- Be honest with the Lord whether we understand His Word.
- Bible truths are to be treasured.
- The New Testament shines light on Old Testament truth, revealing gems.
- Scribes instructed in God's Kingdom know their Bible and skilfully draw on it in the varying circumstances of life.

REFLECTIONS

- Are we honest with the Lord when we do not understand?
- What Bible truths do we really treasure?
- What are the features of a scribe in God's Kingdom?
- What might the old and new treasure be in the Kingdom?

THE EIGHT KINGDOM PARABLES

> **"** *Study to shew thyself approved unto God, a workman that needeth not to be ashamed, rightly dividing the word of truth.* **"**
>
> 2 Timothy 2:15

> **"** *For Ezra had prepared his heart to seek the law of the LORD, and to do it, and to teach in Israel statutes and judgments.* **"**
>
> Ezra 7:10

CONCLUSION

Sons of the Kingdom

The Kingdom is a wonderful theme in our Bible. These eight Kingdom Parables give us beautiful pictures of God's progressive development of His Kingdom. It should inspire us in our princely and priestly service to serve in His Kingdom. The thought of the coming Kingdom when Christ shall reign should motivate us. We are '*sons of the kingdom*'.

Sowers in the Kingdom

These parables should make us walk with dignity, take the seed of God's Word and sow it to all people, and cast the gospel net wide to the whosoever. The Kingdom can only grow through the seed of His Word. We should also remember that the Son of Man is sowing in His own Kingdom: how can the Kingdom not grow?

Scope of the Kingdom

These parables also unfold the mysteries of the Kingdom, revealing a phase of the Kingdom which previously was unknown. This is the period between the two advents of Christ which includes Gentile peoples. We are privileged to get an insight into God's royal dealings with this world now, as seen in the Church period and in the local assembly. We are a royal priesthood, ambassadors for Christ and our citizenship is in heaven.

Satanic attack of the Kingdom

These parables speak of constant opposition from birds, stony soil, thorns, deliberate attacks at night, weeds (tares), covert introduction of error. We should expect that God's Kingdom will constantly be attacked by the Devil.

Strength of the Kingdom

These parables remind us that in the end no satanic attack will have any lasting impact – the field will be furnished with golden grains of wheat, the net will be full of good fish, the treasure, long hidden will be discovered, the pearl of all pearls will be displayed. The Kingdom will be established.

Scribes of the Kingdom

These parables are explained privately to those who enquire and to those who wish to be initiated as scribes of the Kingdom. Let us ensure that we are those who are enjoying the hidden treasures of His Kingdom. Take time to read and reread these parables. May these truths grip our souls and inspire us to greater service for the Lord until He comes. We are training for reigning.

My Notes

CONCLUSION

The Kingdom Parables Overview
(Matthew 13)

NO	Name	Prominent Thought of the Kingdom
1	Sower	Salvation will take place and the seed of God's Word will germinate and true fruit will be evidenced in the life of all who receive it, despite the enemies of God attacking the sowing of the seed.
2	Wheat and Tares	The tares speak of superficiality in God's Kingdom – they are produced through enemy activity, using stealth. This counterfeit Christianity is all exposed by the Lord Jesus and eradicated at the end of the world. The security of the true believer is preserved.
3	Mustard Seed	God blesses a small grain of faith and His Kingdom will substantially grow despite such small beginnings.
4	Leaven hid in Meal	Serious doctrinal error is deliberately introduced into the outward manifestation of the Kingdom on earth and it permeates rapidly amidst the purity of the truth of the Kingdom.
5	Treasure in Field	The treasures of the Kingdom are unseen and then wonderfully discovered through the revelation of faith. The truth of the Kingdom is valued highly, cost God dearly, and remains concealed until the day of revelation.

THE EIGHT KINGDOM PARABLES

6	Pearl of Great Price	The value of the Kingdom is sought diligently until the true priceless value of the Kingdom is discovered. Once discovered, everything else is sold to pay for it. It is all that really matters.
7	Drag Net full of Fish	The scale and variety of people in the professing Kingdom of God is in view. The scope, value, quality and purging of the Kingdom to maintain this purity is emphasised. At the end of the age the Kingdom will contain nothing that offends but be full of diverse types of people who have been saved by the Lord Jesus.
8	The House-holder's Treasure	The Kingdom is like treasure which is scarce (old) as well as modern (new). Selective revelation of the Kingdom treasures can be used to encourage God's people and instruct them in the ways of the Lord.

My Notes

Appendix 1

SEVEN TRANSFORMING CHANGES THAT WILL TAKE PLACE IN THE MILLENNIAL KINGDOM

What significant changes will take place in the Millennium?

1. There will be a spiritual transformation in the world[333].

2. There will be a biological transformation in the animal creation[334].

3. There will be a geographical, topographical, and infrastructural transformation in the world[335].

4. There will be ecological and cosmic transformation[336].

5. There will be political and moral transformation[337].

6. There will be a linguistic transformation, reversing the division of tongues in Babel[338].

7. There will be a social and economic transformation[339].

---

333 Isa. 2.2-3: 'And it shall come to pass in the last days, that the mountain of the LORD'S house shall be established in the top of the mountains, and shall be exalted above the hills; and all nations shall flow unto it. And many people shall go and say, Come ye, and let us go up to the mountain of the LORD, to the house of the God of Jacob; and he will teach us of his ways, and we will walk in his paths: for out of Zion shall go forth the law, and the word of the LORD from Jerusalem';
Ezek. 48.35: 'It was round about eighteen thousand measures: and the name of the city from that day shall be, The LORD is there' (cf. Isa. 11. 9; 66. 23; Zech. 14. 16, 20).
334 Isa. 11.6-7: 'The wolf also shall dwell with the lamb, and the leopard shall lie down with the kid; and the calf and the young lion and the fatling together; and a little child shall lead them. And the cow and the bear shall feed; their young ones shall lie down together: and the lion shall eat straw like the ox';
Isa. 65.20: 'There shall be no more thence an infant of days, nor an old man that hath

not filled his days: for the child shall die an hundred years old; but the sinner being an hundred years old shall be accursed.'

335 Isa 11.15-16: 'And the LORD shall utterly destroy the tongue of the Egyptian sea; and with his mighty wind shall he shake his hand over the river, and shall smite it in the seven streams, and make men go over dryshod. And there shall be an highway for the remnant of his people, which shall be left, from Assyria; like as it was to Israel in the day that he came up out of the land of Egypt';

Zech. 14.4: 'And his feet shall stand in that day upon the mount of Olives, which is before Jerusalem on the east, and the mount of Olives shall cleave in the midst thereof toward the east and toward the west, and there shall be a very great valley; and half of the mountain shall remove toward the north, and half of it toward the south.'

Zech. 14.8-11: 'And it shall be in that day, that living waters shall go out from Jerusalem; half of them toward the former sea, and half of them toward the hinder sea: in summer and in winter shall it be. And the LORD shall be king over all the earth: in that day shall there be one LORD, and his name one. All the land shall be turned as a plain from Geba to Rimmon south of Jerusalem: and it shall be lifted up, and inhabited in her place, from Benjamin's gate unto the place of the first gate, unto the corner gate, and from the tower of Hananeel unto the king's winepresses. And men shall dwell in it, and there shall be no more utter destruction; but Jerusalem shall be safely inhabited';

Isa. 19.23-24: 'In that day shall there be a highway out of Egypt to Assyria, and the Assyrian shall come into Egypt, and the Egyptian into Assyria, and the Egyptians shall serve with the Assyrians. In that day shall Israel be the third with Egypt and with Assyria, even a blessing in the midst of the land:'

336 Isa. 35.1-7: 'The wilderness and the solitary place shall be glad for them; and the desert shall rejoice, and blossom as the rose. It shall blossom abundantly, and rejoice even with joy and singing: the glory of Lebanon shall be given unto it, the excellency of Carmel and Sharon, they shall see the glory of the LORD, and the excellency of our God. Strengthen ye the weak hands, and confirm the feeble knees. Say to them that are of a fearful heart, Be strong, fear not: behold, your God will come with vengeance, even God with a recompense; he will come and save you. Then the eyes of the blind shall be opened, and the ears of the deaf shall be unstopped. Then shall the lame man leap as an hart, and the tongue of the dumb sing: for in the wilderness shall waters break out, and streams in the desert. And the parched ground shall become a pool, and the thirsty land springs of water: in the habitation of dragons, where each lay, shall be grass with reeds and rushes';

Isa. 55.12-13: 'For ye shall go out with joy, and be led forth with peace: the mountains and the hills shall break forth before you into singing, and all the trees of the field shall clap their hands. Instead of the thorn shall come up the fir tree, and instead of the brier shall come up the myrtle tree: and it shall be to the LORD for a name, for an everlasting sign that shall not be cut off.';

Isa. 30.26: 'Moreover the light of the moon shall be as the light of the sun, and the

APPENDIX 1

light of the sun shall be sevenfold, as the light of seven days, in the day that the LORD bindeth up the breach of his people, and healeth the stroke of their wound.'

337 Psalm 72.7-8: 'In his days shall the righteous flourish; and abundance of peace so long as the moon endureth. He shall have dominion also from sea to sea, and from the river unto the ends of the earth';

Isa.11.4: 'But with righteousness shall he judge the poor, and reprove with equity for the meek of the earth ...';

Isa. 66.18-20: 'For I know their works and their thoughts: it shall come, that I will gather all nations and tongues; and they shall come, and see my glory. And I will set a sign among them, and I will send those that escape of them unto the nations, to Tarshish, Pul, and Lud, that draw the bow, to Tubal, and Javan, to the isles afar off, that have not heard my fame, neither have seen my glory; and they shall declare my glory among the Gentiles. And they shall bring all your brethren for an offering unto the LORD out of all nations upon horses, and in chariots, and in litters, and upon mules, and upon swift beasts, to my holy mountain Jerusalem, saith the LORD, as the children of Israel bring an offering in a clean vessel into the house of the LORD.'

338 Isa. 19.18: 'In that day shall five cities in the land of Egypt speak the language of Canaan ...'

339 Psalm 72.12-14: 'For he shall deliver the needy when he crieth; the poor also, and him that hath no helper. He shall spare the poor and needy, and shall save the souls of the needy. He shall redeem their soul from deceit and violence: and precious shall their blood be in his sight';

Isa. 11.12-13: 'And he shall set up an ensign for the nations, and shall assemble the outcasts of Israel, and gather together the dispersed of Judah from the four corners of the earth. The envy also of Ephraim shall depart, and the adversaries of Judah shall be cut off: Ephraim shall not envy Judah, and Judah shall not vex Ephraim';

Isa. 60.17-22: 'For brass I will bring gold, and for iron I will bring silver, and for wood brass, and for stones iron: I will also make thy officers peace, and thine exactors righteousness. Violence shall no more be heard in thy land, wasting nor destruction within thy borders; but thou shalt call thy walls Salvation, and thy gates Praise. The sun shall be no more thy light by day; neither for brightness shall the moon give light unto thee: but the LORD shall be unto thee an everlasting light, and thy God thy glory. Thy sun shall no more go down; neither shall thy moon withdraw itself: for the LORD shall be thine everlasting light, and the days of thy mourning shall be ended. Thy people also shall be all righteous: they shall inherit the land for ever, the branch of my planting, the work of my hands, that I may be glorified. A little one shall become a thousand, and a small one a strong nation: I the LORD will hasten it in his time';

Isa. 65.21: 'And they shall build houses, and inhabit them; and they shall plant vineyards, and eat the fruit of them';

Zech. 14.21: '... and in that day there shall be no more the Canaanite in the house of the LORD of hosts.'

THE EIGHT KINGDOM PARABLES

My Notes

Appendix 2

SEVEN REASONS EXPLAINING WHY THE CHURCH WILL NOT GO THROUGH THE TRIBULATION

(1) No, because the coming of Christ to the air was believed to be imminent.

The early Christians did not anticipate going through a period of extensive world-wide judgment upon earth, because they were expecting the return of Christ at any moment.

- They took the words of Christ at face value[340].

  [It would be strange if the Lord's words were interpreted to mean that they should wait another 2000 years before He returned. That would hardly have been a comfort, as the truth of the coming again of the Lord was intended to be[341].]

- They greeted each other with '*Maranatha*', believing that His coming was soon[342]. John ends the Bible saying, '*Even so, come, Lord Jesus*'[343].

---

340 John 14.1-3: 'Let not your heart be troubled: ye believe in God, believe also in me. In my Father's house are many mansions: if it were not so, I would have told you. I go to prepare a place for you. And if I go and prepare a place for you, I will come again, and receive you unto myself; that where I am, there ye may be also';
John 21.22-23; 'Jesus saith unto him, If I will that he tarry till I come, what is that to thee? follow thou me. Then went this saying abroad among the brethren, that that disciple should not die: yet Jesus said not unto him, He shall not die; but, If I will that he tarry till I come, what is that to thee?'
341 1 Thess. 4.18: 'Wherefore comfort one another with these words.'
342 1 Cor. 16.22 **343** Rev. 22.20

THE EIGHT KINGDOM PARABLES

- They held out to one another the possibility of not dying[344]. Their core belief was, *'we shall not all sleep'*[345].

  [*'After my departing'*, in Acts chapter 20[346], does not mean 'after I die' but 'after I depart the coasts of Ephesus and am no longer physically with you'. Only Peter knew he would die[347]. Paul lived with the possibility of death and resurrection at the same time. It was only right at the end, in 2 Timothy, Paul's last letter, that we learn that Paul knew that he would soon die[348].]

- They comforted each other with the thought of His imminent coming[349], saying it was a *'little while'*[350].

- They regarded the first evidence of salvation to be found *'waiting for his Son from heaven'*[351]. Looking for Him became the Christian's occupation[352]. This would be unusual behaviour if it were accepted that His coming could not take place until after a world-wide apostasy some millennia in the future.

---

344 2 Cor. 5.1-2: 'For we know that if [please notice the 'if' – it was a possibility that their earthly house (their body) need not be dissolved and they be naked in death, but clothed upon] our earthly house of this tabernacle were dissolved, we have a building of God, an house not made with hands, eternal in the heavens. For in this we groan, earnestly desiring to be clothed upon with our house which is from heaven:'

345 1 Cor. 15.51: 'Behold, I shew you a mystery; We shall not all sleep, but we shall all be changed'

346 Acts 20.29

347 John 21.18-19: 'Verily, verily, I say unto thee, When thou wast young, thou girdedst thyself, and walkedst whither thou wouldest: but when thou shalt be old, thou shalt stretch forth thy hands, and another shall gird thee, and carry thee whither thou wouldest not. This spake he, signifying by what death he should glorify God. And when he had spoken this, he saith unto him, Follow me.'

348 2 Tim. 4.6: 'For I am now ready to be offered, and the time of my departure is at hand.'

349 1 Thess. 4.13-18: 'But I would not have you to be ignorant, brethren, concerning them which are asleep, that ye sorrow not, even as others which have no hope. For if we believe that Jesus died and rose again, even so them also which sleep in Jesus will God bring with him. For this we say unto you by the word of the Lord, that we which are alive and remain unto the coming of the Lord shall not prevent them which are asleep. For the Lord himself shall descend from heaven with a shout, with the voice of the archangel, and with the trump of God: and the dead in Christ shall rise first: Then

APPENDIX 2

- They warned against behaviour that would be unbecoming at His return[353].

(2) No, because the structure of the book of Revelation does not allow it

Revelation 6 to 18 is the Tribulation period, and the Church is not mentioned once in this section, despite the fact that the book is written to the 7 Churches[354]. After chapter 3 we never read again of the Church, until we see her coming out of heaven in chapter 19. Almost in every chapter in this section (Chapters 4 - 18) we can see things which would exclude us. Can we pray the prayer of Rev. 6. 10?[355] That prayer is not how our Lord prayed in Luke 23. 34![356] In Revelation 7 there are two groups of people, Jews and Gentiles, quite distinct, but in the Church God has *made in himself of two one new man*[357]. There are no such distinctions in the Church. Additionally, in Rev. 19. 1-10 the Church is in heaven before the return of Christ to earth. The Lord comes as King of Kings out of Heaven

we which are alive and remain shall be caught up together with them in the clouds, to meet the Lord in the air: and so shall we ever be with the Lord. Wherefore comfort one another with these words.'

350 Heb. 10.37: 'For yet a little while, and he that shall come will come, and will not tarry.'

351 1 Thess. 1.10

352 Tit. 2.13: 'Looking for that blessed hope, and the glorious appearing of the great God and our Saviour Jesus Christ';
Heb. 9.28: 'So Christ was once offered to bear the sins of many; and unto them that look for him shall he appear the second time without sin unto salvation.'

353 1 John 2.28: 'And now, little children, abide in him; that, when he shall appear, we may have confidence, and not be ashamed before him at his coming.'

354 Rev. 1.4: 'John to the seven churches which are in Asia: Grace be unto you, and peace, from him which is, and which was, and which is to come; and from the seven Spirits which are before his throne.'

355 Rev. 6.10: 'And they cried with a loud voice, saying, How long, O Lord, holy and true, dost thou not judge and avenge our blood on them that dwell on the earth?'

356 Luke 23.34: 'Then said Jesus, Father, forgive them; for they know not what they do. And they parted his raiment, and cast lots.'

357 Eph. 2.15: 'Having abolished in his flesh the enmity, even the law of commandments contained in ordinances; for to make in himself of twain one new man, so making peace;'

THE EIGHT KINGDOM PARABLES

to reign from verse 11 onwards in this chapter[358]. But the Church (the bride) is in Heaven clothed in righteousness from verses 1-10. How did she get there? She was transported there beforehand. When the world is cursing God for His judgments[359], the Church will be in heaven with Christ.

(3) No, because the New Testament explicitly teaches the reverse

To the Church at Philadelphia:

'I also will keep thee from ['out from' – i.e. never in it] *the hour of temptation* [Tribulation], *which shall come upon all the world, to try them that dwell upon the earth. Behold, I come quickly'*[360].

To the Church at Thessalonica:

'For God hath not appointed us to [Tribulation] *wrath, but to obtain salvation by our Lord Jesus Christ'*;[361]

'Now we beseech you, brethren, by the coming of our Lord Jesus Christ, and by our gathering together unto him [i.e. His return to the air], *that ye be not soon shaken in mind, or be troubled, neither by spirit, nor by word, nor by letter as from us, as that the day of Christ* [better, with the majority of manuscripts, 'the Lord'] *is at hand'*[362].

---

358 Rev. 19.1-11: 'And after these things I heard a great voice of much people in heaven, saying, Alleluia; Salvation, and glory, and honour, and power, unto the Lord our God: For true and righteous are his judgments: for he hath judged the great whore, which did corrupt the earth with her fornication, and hath avenged the blood of his servants at her hand. And again they said, Alleluia. And her smoke rose up for ever and ever. And the four and twenty elders and the four beasts fell down and worshipped God that sat on the throne, saying, Amen; Alleluia. And a voice came out of the throne, saying, Praise our God, all ye his servants, and ye that fear him, both small and great. And I heard as it were the voice of a great multitude, and as the voice of many waters, and as the voice of mighty thunderings, saying, Alleluia: for the Lord God omnipotent reigneth. Let us be glad and rejoice, and give honour to him: for the marriage of the Lamb is come, and his wife hath made herself ready. And to her was granted that she should be arrayed in fine linen, clean and white: for the fine linen is the righteousness of saints. And he saith unto me, Write, Blessed are they which are called unto the marriage supper of the Lamb. And he saith unto me, These are the true sayings of

APPENDIX 2

Paul explicitly taught that the day of the Lord, which definitely encompasses the Tribulation period, would come after the apostasy had taken place'[363]. The Thessalonian saints need not be worried and concerned by reports that this day had commenced; they were to look for the Lord from Heaven instead: they were safe from this Tribulation wrath.

(4) No, because otherwise the imagery of the Old Testament would be lost

The Rapture is prefigured in the life of Joseph: Joseph married Asenath in Genesis 41. Joseph, a picture of the Saviour, did this before the seven years of famine and the time of testing of his brethren in chapters 42-47 of Genesis. We do not read of Asenath in these times of famine or trial. This is a beautiful picture of the Church escaping the seven years of *'Tribulation which will come on all the earth'*[364]. Enoch was taken up to glory alive before the judgments of the flood in Noah's day:[365] this is a picture of the saints being raptured prior to the judgment of God on earth. Abraham was up in the height of Hebron (picture of heaven) and was spared the wrath that fell upon Lot down in the plains of Sodom (picture of earth)[366]. While this New Testament truth is not explicitly taught in the Old Testament, it seems likely that God has left pictures latent in the Old Testament Scriptures for us to enjoy. They do not prove the point, but they are consistent with the New Testament teaching.

God. And I fell at his feet to worship him. And he said unto me, See thou do t not: I am thy fellow servant, and of thy brethren that have the testimony of Jesus: worship God: for the testimony of Jesus is the spirit of prophecy. And I saw heaven opened, and behold a white horse; and he that sat upon him was called Faithful and True, and in righteousness he doth judge and make war.'

359 Rev. 16. 11: 'And blasphemed the God of heaven because of their pains and their sores, and repented not of their deeds.'

360 Rev. 3.10-11 **361** 1 Thess. 5.9 **362** 2 Thess. 2.1-2

363 2 Thess. 2.3: 'let no man deceive you by any means: for that day shall not come, except there come a falling away first, and that man of sin be revealed, the son of perdition'.

364 Rev. 3.10

365 Gen. 5.24: 'And Enoch walked with God: and he was not; for God took him.'
366 Gen. 19.27-28

(5) No, because the general flow of prophecy demands otherwise.

The general flow of prophecy in the New Testament is as follows: Israel has been set aside[367], whilst Gentiles are brought in[368]. Israel, however, will be taken up again (*'graft in again'*) once the Church is taken away. The Church is something new[369] and not an extension of Israel. By insisting that the Church goes through the Tribulation it removes the distinction of the Church and Israel and seems to run counter to this general pattern of prophecy.

(6) No, because the "gaps" in Scripture suggest otherwise

- Our Lord stopped halfway through a sentence when reading Isaiah 61 verse 2, as recorded in Luke 4. 16-20[370]. He knew the difference

---

367 Matt. 21.43: 'Therefore say I unto you, The kingdom of God shall be taken from you, and given to a nation bringing forth the fruits thereof.'

368 Romans 11. 11-26: 'I say then, Have they stumbled that they should fall? God forbid: but rather through their fall salvation is come unto the Gentiles, for to provoke them to jealousy. Now if the fall of them be the riches of the world, and the diminishing of them the riches of the Gentiles; how much more their fulness? For I speak to you Gentiles, inasmuch as I am the apostle of the Gentiles, I magnify mine office. If by any means I may provoke to emulation them which are my flesh, and might save some of them. For if the casting away of them be the reconciling of the world, what shall the receiving of them be, but life from the dead? For if the firstfruit be holy, the lump is also holy: and if the root be holy, so are the branches. And if some of the branches be broken off, and thou, being a wild olive tree, wert graffed in among them, and with them partakest of the root and fatness of the olive tree; Boast not against the branches. But if thou boast, thou bearest not the root, but the root thee. Thou wilt say then, The branches were broken off, that I might be graffed in. Well; because of unbelief they were broken off, and thou standest by faith. Be not highminded, but fear: For if God spared not the natural branches, take heed lest he also spare not thee. Behold therefore the goodness and severity of God: on them which fell, severity; but toward thee, goodness, if thou continue in his goodness: otherwise thou also shalt be cut off. And they also, if they abide not still in unbelief, shall be graffed in: for God is able to graff them in again. For if thou wert cut out of the olive tree which is wild by nature, and wert graffed contrary to nature into a good olive tree: how much more shall these, which be the natural branches, be graffed into their own olive tree? For I would not, brethren, that ye should be ignorant of this mystery, lest ye should be wise

between the 'acceptable year of the Lord' (Church period) and the 'day of vengeance' (Daniel's 70th week). These events do not blend into one another.

- The gap between the 69 weeks (Dan 9. 24-26[371]) and the 70th week of Daniel's prophecy (Dan. 9. 27[372]).

- The gap between Zechariah 9. 9 and Zechariah 9. 10[373].

- The gap between Isaiah 52. 14 and 52. 15[374].

(7) No, because otherwise the Scriptures would be contradictory

The New Testament teaches that 'we shall **all** be changed'[375] at the Rapture, that is, that we will all have resurrection bodies[376], in which there

in your own conceits; that blindness in part is happened to Israel, until the fulness of the Gentiles be come in. And so all Israel shall be saved: as it is written, There shall come out of Sion the Deliverer, and shall turn away ungodliness from Jacob'.

369 Eph. 2.15 (note the word 'new') and Matt. 16. 18 (note the word 'will' i.e. something future and not made out of the old material of Israel).

370 Isa 61.1-2: 'The Spirit of the Lord GOD is upon me; because the LORD hath anointed me to preach good tidings unto the meek; he hath sent me to bind up the brokenhearted, to proclaim liberty to the captives, and the opening of the prison to them that are bound; To proclaim the acceptable year of the LORD, and the day of vengeance of our God; to comfort all that mourn;'

371 Dan 9.24-26: 'Seventy weeks are determined upon thy people and upon thy holy city, to finish the transgression, and to make an end of sins, and to make reconciliation for iniquity, and to bring in everlasting righteousness, and to seal up the vision and prophecy, and to anoint the most Holy. Know therefore and understand, that from the going forth of the commandment to restore and to build Jerusalem unto the Messiah the Prince shall be seven weeks, and threescore and two weeks: the street shall be built again, and the wall, even in troublous times. And after threescore and two weeks shall Messiah be cut off, but not for himself: and the people of the prince that shall come shall destroy the city and the sanctuary; and the end thereof shall be with a flood, and unto the end of the war desolations are determined.'

372 Dan. 9.27: 'And he shall confirm the covenant with many for one week: and in the midst of the week he shall cause the sacrifice and the oblation to cease, and for the overspreading of abominations he shall make it desolate, even until the consummation, and that determined shall be poured upon the desolate.'

THE EIGHT KINGDOM PARABLES

is 'neither marrying nor giving in marriage'[377] (teaching of the Lord Jesus to the Sadducees). At the Rapture, the dead saints are raised **before** living saints are changed, both meeting in the air at the same time[378]. However, in the Old Testament prophetic Scriptures it would seem as if the dead saints are raised **after** the return of Christ, to join the living saints on earth[379]. There are many examples in Scripture to uphold the fact that the Church will all have resurrected bodies at the Rapture[380], but we know of no Scripture to show that living saints on earth who survive the Tribulation will have their bodies changed into a "resurrection body" when the Lord comes in glory. Indeed, the fact that children will be born during the Millennium precludes it. The truth that *we shall **all** be changed* can only be true at the Rapture. It cannot be true at the manifestation, as there will still be death in the Millennium so not all will have resurrection

---

373 Zech. 9.9: ' Rejoice greatly, O daughter of Zion; shout, O daughter of Jerusalem: behold, thy King cometh unto thee: he is just, and having salvation; lowly, and riding upon an ass, and upon a colt the foal of an ass';
Zech. 9.10: 'And I will cut off the chariot from Ephraim, and the horse from Jerusalem, and the battle bow shall be cut off: and he shall speak peace unto the heathen: and his dominion shall be from sea even to sea, and from the river even to the ends of the earth.'
374 Isa. 52.14: 'As many were astonied at thee; his visage was so marred more than any man, and his form more than the sons of men';
Isa. 52.15: 'So shall he sprinkle many nations; the kings shall shut their mouths at him: for that which had not been told them shall they see; and that which they had not heard shall they consider.'
375 1 Cor. 15.51
376 Phil. 3.20-21: ' For our conversation is in heaven; from whence also we look for the Saviour, the Lord Jesus Christ: Who shall change our vile body, that it may be fashioned like unto his glorious body, according to the working whereby he is able even to subdue all things unto himself.'
377 Matt. 22.30: 'For in the resurrection they neither marry, nor are given in marriage, but are as the angels of God in heaven.'
378 1 Thess. 4.15-17: 'For this we say unto you by the word of the Lord, that we which are alive and remain unto the coming of the Lord shall not prevent them which are asleep. For the Lord himself shall descend from heaven with a shout, with the voice of the archangel, and with the trump of God: and the dead in Christ shall rise first: Then we which are alive and remain shall be caught up together with them in the clouds, to meet the Lord in the air: and so shall we ever be with the Lord.'
379 Dan 11.45-12.3: 'And he [Man of Sin] shall plant the tabernacles of his palace between the seas in the glorious holy mountain; yet he shall come to his end, and none

APPENDIX 2

bodies in the Millennium[381]. It is the children born to these people that will be part of the rebellion at the end of the Millennium[382]. By insisting that the Church goes through the Tribulation and that the return of Christ for the Church to the air (Rapture) and the manifestation of Christ to the earth happen at the same time makes these prophetic Scriptures contradictory. The *scripture cannot be broken*'[383].

My Notes

---

shall help him. And at that time shall Michael stand up, the great prince which standeth for the children of thy people: and there shall be a time of trouble, such as never was since there was a nation even to that same time: and at that time thy people shall be delivered, every one that shall be found written in the book. And many of them that sleep in the dust of the earth shall awake, some to everlasting life, and some to shame and everlasting contempt. And they that be wise shall shine as the brightness of the firmament; and they that turn many to righteousness as the stars for ever and ever'; Matt. 8.11: 'And I say unto you, That many shall come from the east and west, and shall sit down with Abraham, and Isaac, and Jacob, in the kingdom of heaven.'

380 Phil. 3.21: 'Who shall change our vile body, that it may be fashioned like unto his glorious body, according to the working whereby he is able even to subdue all things unto himself.'

381 Zech. 14.17-19: 'And it shall be, that whoso will not come up of all the families of the earth unto Jerusalem to worship the King, the LORD of hosts, even upon them shall be no rain. And if the family of Egypt go not up, and come not, that have no rain; there shall be the plague, wherewith the LORD will smite the heathen that come not up to keep the feast of tabernacles. This shall be the punishment of Egypt, and the punishment of all nations that come not up to keep the feast of tabernacles.'

382 Rev. 20.7-9: 'And when the thousand years are expired, Satan shall be loosed out of his prison, And shall go out to deceive the nations which are in the four quarters of the earth, Gog and Magog, to gather them together to battle: the number of whom is as the sand of the sea. And they went up on the breadth of the earth, and compassed the camp of the saints about, and the beloved city: and fire came down from God out of heaven, and devoured them.'

383 John 10.35

The Second Coming of Christ for the Church and for Judgment

The Return to the Air	The Return to the Earth
New Revelation in New Testament **Returns for the Church** (1 Cor. 15. 51; 1 Thess. 4. 15)	*Revealed in Old and New Testament* **Returns for the Kingdom** (Zech. 14; Matt..24; 2 Thess. 2)
Comparison • Marks the end of the Church period and the beginning of Daniel's 70th week*. (1 Thess. 5. 9; 2 Thess. 2. 1-6; Rev. 3. 10; Compare Rev. Ch. 2-3 with Ch. 4-19) • The "Fullness of the Gentiles" complete (Rom 11.25) • The change of body will come in the twinkling of an eye (1 Cor. 15. 52) • Resurrection of all "in Christ" [i.e., the Church – 1 Thess. 4:16] * (although there could well be a transition period before the Tribulation period commences)	**Comparison** • Marks the end of Daniel's 70th week and the beginning of the Kingdom period (Dan. 9. 27; 2 Thess. 2. 3-8; Matt. 24. 15 Dan. 2. 44; Matt. 24. 31; Zech. 14. 9) • The "Times of the Gentiles" concluded (Luke 21. 24) • Will come like a thief in the night (Matt. 24. 43-44; 1 Thess. 5. 3) • Resurrection of all who "are Christ's" [i.e. OT saints, Tribulation saints 1Cor. 15. 23; Dan. 12. 2; Matt. 8. 11; Rev. 6. 9-11; 7. 14]
Contrast • Returns to the Air (1 Thess. 4. 17) • Dead saints raised before living saints are changed, meeting in the air (1 Thess. 4. 15-17) • Blessing for the Church: "Comfort" (1 Thess. 4. 16-18) • Expected at any moment (Rev. 3. 11; 22. 20; Heb. 10. 37; 2 Cor. 5. 1; 1 Cor. 15. 51-52; 2 Thess. 2. 1)	**Contrast** • Returns to the Earth (Zech .14. 4) • Dead saints raised after the return of Christ to join the living saints on earth (Zech. 14. 14; Dan. 11. 45-12. 3). No record of living saints being changed. • Vengeance on Enemies (2 Thess. 1. 8) • Expected after the apostasy of the man of sin (2 Thess. 2. 3-6) • Comes accompanied with Angels

Appendix 3

THE KINGDOM OF GOD AND THE KINGDOM OF HEAVEN

The Kingdom of God is the place of God's overarching sovereign rule[384]. However, Satan has a *'Kingdom'* too and he is currently permitted by God a sphere of rule[385]. Daniel also taught us that civil rulers over significant jurisdictions are permitted to rule by God: *'that the most High ruleth in the kingdom of men, and giveth it to whomsoever he will, and setteth up over it the basest of men'*[386]. So that the Kingdom that God presides over is the totality of everything, even when wicked men are permitted to rule. God is sovereign in the universe. Challenging this sovereignty is the Kingdom of evil, overseen by Satan, who will ultimately be destroyed.

Under this umbrella term, the universal 'Kingdom of God', however, there are various phases of the 'Kingdom'. We have already seen that Israel, the Church, Tribulation remnant and a future restored world-wide Kingdom on earth are all part of the expression of the Kingdom of God, but not one of these phases of the Kingdom is the totality of it (see diagram in chapter 4). This means, for example, that the Church is in the Kingdom, but the Church is not the totality of the Kingdom. Neither is the Millennial Kingdom the totality of the Kingdom, given that failure exists within it. That awaits the new heavens and the new earth where righteousness dwells and then, and only then, will the Kingdom be perfected.

Seventy-two times we read of the Kingdom of God in the New Testament, and thirty-two times the Kingdom of Heaven, all of which are found in the Gospel of Matthew. Other related expressions to the 'Kingdom' are found in the following references:

- Matt. 6. 10 (*'Thy Kingdom'*)
- 2 Tim. 4. 18 (*'heavenly Kingdom'*)

---

384 1 Chron. 29.11-12 **385** Matt. 12.26 **386** Dan. 4.17

THE EIGHT KINGDOM PARABLES

- Col. 1.13 ('*Kingdom of his dear Son*' ['the Son of his love'])
- Eph. 5. 5 ('*Kingdom of Christ and of God*')
- Matt. 26. 29 ('*my Father's Kingdom*')
- 2 Pet. 1. 11 ('*the everlasting Kingdom of our Lord and Saviour*')
- John 18. 36; Luke 22. 30 ('*My Kingdom*')

Therefore, the Scriptures clearly reveal a Kingdom on earth for a thousand years, in which Christ will reign prior to the eternal state – read Revelation 20. 1-21. 5. They also transparently show that the rule of God is also part and parcel of salvation, existing in the hearts and lives of those who put their trust in Jesus Christ (Col. 1. 13). Christ has a Kingdom now which is '*not of this world*'[387]. However, not all agree on how the Kingdom of God is manifested today and whether there is any difference between the Kingdom of God and the Kingdom of Heaven. We therefore go forward on this topic cautiously, looking at what is revealed in Scripture.

The table opposite summarises the **common features** of the Kingdom of God and the Kingdom of Heaven:

My Notes

---

[387] John 18.36

APPENDIX 3

Common Features: Kingdom of Heaven and the Kingdom of God

Kingdom of Heaven	Kingdom of God
The 'Kingdom of Heaven is at hand' is preached by John the Baptist and the Lord Jesus (Matt. 3.2; 4.17; 10.7)	... so is the Kingdom of God (Mark 1. 14-15; Luke 10.9, 11; 11.20; 21.31)
The Kingdom of Heaven is a blessing enjoyed now by the poor in spirit, the righteous and those who do the will of God (Matt. 5. 3, 10; 19-20; 7. 21).	... so is the Kingdom of God (Luke 6. 20; 1 Cor. 6. 9-10; Gal. 5. 21; Eph. 5. 5; 2 Thess. 1. 5);
The Kingdom of Heaven includes Gentiles in a future day (Matt. 8. 11)	... so does the Kingdom of God (Luke 13. 29)
The Kingdom of Heaven is growing (Matt. 13.1-32)	... so is the Kingdom of God (Mark 4. 30-32; Luke 13. 18-19).
The Kingdom of Heaven comes under satanic attack (Matt. 13. 31-32)	... so does the Kingdom of God (Mark 4. 30-32; Luke 13. 19
The Kingdom of Heaven has leaven, symbolic of corrupt doctrine, within it (Matt. 13. 33)	... so does the Kingdom of God (Luke 13. 20-21)
The Kingdom of Heaven is difficult to enter due to covetousness, religious pride etc. (Matt. 19. 23; 23. 13)	... so is the Kingdom of God (Mark 10. 23-25; Luke 18. 24-25; John 3. 5; Acts 14. 22);
Some of the features of the Kingdom of Heaven are "mysteries" (Matt. 13. 11)	... so, also in the Kingdom of God (Mark 4. 11; Luke 8. 10)
The Kingdom of Heaven is likened unto children (Matt. 19. 14)	... so is the Kingdom of God (Mark 10. 14-15; Luke 18. 16-17)

The table on the next page summarises the **contrasting features** of the Kingdom of God and the Kingdom of Heaven:

Contrasting Features: Kingdom of Heaven and the Kingdom of God

Kingdom of Heaven	Kingdom of God
The expression Kingdom of Heaven is confined to Matthew's Gospel.	On six occasions Matthew uses the expression Kingdom of God. These are worthy of consideration to show the distinction between these two very similar terms.
The Kingdom of Heaven includes those who profess to be saved but are shown to be false and are removed when the Lord Jesus comes (Matt. 13. 24-30, 36-43, 47-50; 22. 1-14; 25. 1-11)	The Kingdom of God includes only those born again, saved (John 3. 3, 5) and excludes the unsaved (Mark 4. 26-29: there is no parable of tares]; Mark 9:47 [Note the Kingdom of God contrasted to hell]; Luke 13.18-19; cp. also Luke 13.23 with Luke 13.28-29; Luke 18. 24-26)
The Kingdom of Heaven includes falsehood (Matt. 13. 24-30, 33)	The Kingdom of God is characterized by righteousness, peace, and joy in the Holy Spirit (Rom. 14. 17). The Kingdom of God is inherited only by incorruptible beings (1 Cor. 15. 50).

The two terms are therefore almost identical, but not quite. The Kingdom of God only includes the saved and the Kingdom of Heaven also includes those who claim to be saved. The Kingdom of God requires you to be born again; in contrast, the Kingdom of Heaven includes the sphere of profession: the parable of the Wheat and Tares and the parable of the Dragnet display this, with the separation of wheat from tares only coming at the time of harvest and the separating of the fish on the shore only after the boat has been beached. These parables are a picture of profession: the tares look like the wheat, but their true character will be revealed at the final judgment; the dragnet, which is compared to the Kingdom of Heaven, gathers up fish of every kind: those fish gathered into the net are not separated until the final judgment or the harvest. The 'bad fish' which are eventually removed represent the sphere of profession – those who

APPENDIX 3

claim to belong to Christ but are not real – since they are distinguished from all other fish in the sea by the fact that they are in the net.

The Kingdom of God in the Gospel of Matthew

It is of interest that, while Matthew normally uses the expression Kingdom of Heaven, there are six possible cases where the use of the word 'Kingdom' in Matthew refers to the Kingdom of God rather than to the Kingdom of Heaven.

Ref.	Kingdom of God	Explanation
Matt. 6.33	But seek ye first the Kingdom of God, and his righteousness; and all these things shall be added unto you.	The Kingdom here refers to the sphere of salvation only
Matt. 12:28	But if I cast out devils by the Spirit of God, then the Kingdom of God is come unto you.	Indicates the reality of the power of the true Kingdom of God.
Matt. 13.38	...the good seed are the children of the Kingdom; but the tares are the children of the wicked one;	This is the true Kingdom. If it had said the Kingdom of Heaven, it would have destroyed the contrast with the Devil's evil Kingdom.
Matt. 13.43	Then shall the righteous shine forth as the sun in the Kingdom of their Father	Only the truly righteous will shine in the Kingdom. There is no thought of falsehood here.
Matt. 19.24	And again I say unto you, It is easier for a camel to go through the eye of a needle, than for a rich man to enter into the Kingdom of God	This Kingdom is the sphere of salvation, as the disciples respond in the next verse with: who then can be saved?
Matt. 21.43	Therefore say I unto you, The Kingdom of God shall be taken from you, and given to a nation bringing forth the fruits thereof.	The only meaning this can have is the true Kingdom where true fruit will be seen: no thought of profession here.

It is most significant that Matthew goes out of his way to use the expression *'kingdom of God'* whenever the reality of true salvation is required.

Conclusion

There is evidence that while the Kingdom of Heaven is similar in many respects to the Kingdom of God and in some contexts they seem to be used synonymously, in others the Kingdom of Heaven is contrasted to the Kingdom of God. The Kingdom of God includes all who truly belong to the Lord, whether in heaven or earth. The Kingdom of Heaven seems to be limited to the earthly sphere and excludes angels and other creatures but includes all those who profess salvation and who are outwardly identified with God, whether they are saved or not.

Although scholars will continue to differ on this point, a careful exegesis of the passages on the Kingdom of Heaven seems to confirm the thought that the Kingdom of Heaven is a sphere of profession of eternal life, in contrast to the Kingdom of God as the sphere of possession of eternal life.